Focus on Proficiency

Teacher's Book

Sue O'Connell

**REVISED AND ENLARGED EDITION
WITH EXAM PRACTICE MATERIAL**

COLLINS E•L•T
London and Glasgow

UNIT BY UNIT PLAN

	Lead-in	Texts	Listening	Comm. Activity	Grammar	Writing	Exam Practice	Study Boxes
1 HOMES	Contrasting homes — description/ discussion	1. Finding friends 2. Tower slums Register: 4 extracts	A house in Sana'a Home Improvements (end section)	Role play: estate agent and house buyer (pairs)	The passive voice	1. Description of a house 2. Letter of complaint 3. Description of process	Vocab. practice 1. Review 2. Verbs describing movement of liquid Grammar practice	Study Box (SB) Language Check (LC) 1. SB Letter writing 2. LC Dep Preps 1: verb + preposition
2 WORK	Job satisfaction — discussion	1. The clerk 2. Equal at work? Register: 4 job advertisements	Job interview Time is money (end section)	Clothes to wear at work (pairs)	1. Review of present perfect 2. Phrasal verbs	Narrative/ Descriptive	Vocab. practice 1. Review 2. Phrasal verb: take Grammar practice	1. SB Stative verbs 2. LC do vs make
3 TOURIST OR TRAVELLER	Photographs — description/ discussion	1. Travel 2. Amateur photography Register: 4 extracts about New York	1. Holiday Scene — radio programme 2. Holiday Caravans Himalayan Kingdoms (end section)	The desert survival problem (groups)	1. Not only.. but also... (inversion) 2. Review of conditionals 1 and 2.	Directed writing (letter)	Vocab. practice 1. Review 2. Verbs describing facial expression Grammar practice	1. LC Dep preps 2: preposition + noun 2. SB prevent vs avoid 3. SB Phrasal verbs 1: give out, give off, cut out, allow for, get down to
4 RELATIONSHIPS	1. Quiz: relationships in Britain 2. Reading: What makes marriage tick? What is a close friend?	1. Quarelling 2. Neighbours Register: 3 sections from a magazine	The launderette — radio documentary	Self assertion (pairs)	Modal verbs for Permission and Probability	1. Discussion 2. Narrative/ Descriptive	Vocab. practice 1. Review 2. The suffix 'some' 3. The suffix 'ate' Grammar practice	1. SB sue vs prosecute 2. LC Dep preps 3: adjective + preposition
5 HEALTH	Health Risks — discussion	1. Why do we still dice with death? 2. Hypochondriacs arise 3. Angels in hell Register: 4 extracts on cycling theme	Keep fit class A many-sided therapy (end section)	Fitness project (pairs)	1. Review of conditional 3 2. If only.... (wishes and regrets)	1. Instructions 2. Discussion	Vocab. practice 1. Review 2. Expressions for ill health and injury. Grammar practice	1. SB Expressing concession: part one and two 2. SB Phrasal verbs 2: carry out, carry on, set up, (go on), give up

	Lead-in	Texts	Listening	Comm. Activity	Grammar	Writing	Exam Practice	Study Boxes
6 CRIME & PUNISHMENT	Quiz: Crime and Punishment in Britain	1. Hoisting 2. Everyone needs a guardian angel Register: headlines	Security devices - radio report Another crime statistic (end section)	Alibi (pairs)	1. Gerunds 2. The infinitive 3. Gerund vs infinitive	1. Narrative/descriptive 2. Discussion	Vocab. practice 1. Review 2. Phrasal verb: get Grammar practice	1. SB Phrasal verbs 3: join up, set off, cut off, break in 2. SB accuse of vs charge with 3. LC Dep preps 4: verb + preposition
7 LEARNING & TEACHING	Pictures: description/discussion	1. The teenage teachers 2. An education for life 3. Twilight of the history man Register: 3 extracts on theme of computers	Open University student — interview Acquiring new skills (end section)	Which evening class? role play (pairs)	1. Defining and non-defining relative clauses 2. 'ing' forms	1. Report based on statistics 2. Instructions	Vocab. practice 1. Review 2. Expressions using animal names Grammar practice	1. LC Dep Preps 5: adjective + preposition 2. SB Summary writing 3. SB Phrasal verbs 4: set (up) on, take to, put off, go about, put across, send up.
8 THE MEDIA	Pictures and discussion points	1. Illusions of power 2. A medium of no importance Register: Headlines and texts	Guided tour of TV studio Your friendly local station (end section)	Radio interview-role play (groups)	1. Expressing future time 2. Present tenses for future	Discussion	Vocab practice 1. Review 2. Phrasal verb: put Grammar practice	1. SB Phrasal verbs 5: go down, go off, come up with, turn out 2. LC Just
9 SCIENCE & TECHNOLOGY	Inventions — description/discussion	1. Does technology work backwards? 2. Spanner in the robot's works 3. The price of progress Register: Could this product kill millions?	1. The world's most valuable mineral 2. The salterns of Brittany	The description game (pairs)	Modal verbs for Ability and Obligation	1. Description 2. Discussion	Vocab. practice 1. Review 2. Phrasal verb: set 3. The prefix 'out' Grammar practice	1. LC Dep preps 6: preposition + nouns 2. SB Phrasal verbs 6: work out, take over, break up
10 THE CONSUMER SOCIETY	Advertisements — description/discussion/comparison	1. The development of advertising 2. A marketing revolution 3. The strange new taste of tomorrow Register: consumer's guide to 4 pets	Consumer affairs-radio programme Something to complain about (end section)	Consumer law quiz (pairs)	Review of reported speech	1. Discussion 2. Report	Vocab. practice 1. Review 2. Phrasal verb: come Grammar practice	1. SB actual vs actually 2. LC suffixes

CONTENTS

INTRODUCTION

Focus on Proficiency is a complete course which provides thorough practice for the compulsory sections of each of the five papers of the *Cambridge Certificate of Proficiency in English* examination.

The aim throughout has been to balance the systematic development of the skills required to pass the examination with the provision of the necessary practice material in the examination format.

Key aspects of the examination include the wide variety of text types, both listening and reading, the high proportion of authentic material, the realistic communication tasks and the relatively high weighting of the listening and oral components (one third of the total marks).

Each of these aspects has been taken fully into account in *Focus on Proficiency*. There is a very wide range of reading texts, all taken from newspapers, magazines or non-fiction works. The majority of the listening texts are based on authentic material, and the listening tasks themselves are extremely varied. A number of the communication activities and lead-ins are also authentic in that they were designed originally for native speakers. There is also a special emphasis on student interaction throughout the book. Communication activities are a feature of each unit and these include problem solving and information gap exercises which have been designed to be both enjoyable and motivating.

With this revised and enlarged edition of *Focus on Proficiency*, the opportunity has arisen to incorporate a number of improvements suggested in feedback from teachers and students using the course throughout the world. The main addition is the inclusion of an Exam Practice section at the back of the book which provides extra practice for Papers 4 and 5 (the Listening and Interview papers). In addition, Study Boxes dealing with phrasal verbs, dependent prepositions and other aspects of language which are regularly tested in the examination have been introduced. Futher improvements include the new design in a larger format, with a second colour for greater clarity. There is more visual material than previously. Last but by no means least, the book now includes a much requested index!

The requirements of the examination, in detail, are as follows:

PAPER 1   Reading Comprehension (1 hour)   40 marks

A 25 multiple-choice questions designed to test vocabulary and formal grammatical control, in sentence contexts.
B 15 multiple-choice questions based on three or more texts, designed to test gist and detailed content, recognition of form, register and intention.

PAPER 2   Composition (2 hours)   40 marks

Two compositions from a choice of descriptive, situational or discursive topics.*

Assessment is based on organisation and clarity of content, accuracy of grammatical control, fluency and range of expression.

PAPER 3   Use of English (2 hours)   40 marks

A Open-completion of transformation items designed to test active control of the patterns and usage of English.
B Questions on a passage designed to test ability to understand, interpret and summarise.

PAPER 4   Listening Comprehension   20 marks
(approx 30 mins)

Questions of varying type (selection, re-ordering, blank-filling etc.) to test accurate understanding of spoken English, based on recorded material.

PAPER 5   Interview (approx 15 minutes)   40 marks

Based on a picture stimulus, and related passages and other material. The interview may, optionally, be conducted in groups of two or three candidates.

*Set texts may be chosen as the basis for one of the topics in Paper 2 and for the communication exercise in Paper 5. As these change every two years, they are not included in this practice material.

Assessment is based on fluency and grammatical accuracy, pronunciation (individual sounds, and stress and linking of phrases), communicative ability and vocabulary.

HOW TO USE THE COURSE

The course consists of ten units, each containing the same component sections which cover all five of the Proficiency papers. The order of the sections varies to some extent from unit to unit, as does the degree of attention to each component within a unit. Unit 1, for example, has three Focus on writing sections, one Focus on grammar and one Focus on listening, while other units may reflect a different balance.

Each unit has an 'umbrella' topic and contains materials relating to several loosely-related sub-topics. Unit 5 'Health', for example, covers a variety of issues including health risks, hypochondria, stress in the nursing profession, keep-fit exercises and cycling. There are frequently 'clusters' of sections which are closely connected. In Unit 5, for example, the Lead-in and Focus on grammar 1 relate directly to Text 1, Focus on grammar 2 relates to Text 2, and Focus on writing relates to Focus on listening.

The materials in each unit can and should be used fairly flexibly to meet the needs of the particular teaching situation and class. For example, after the initial 'cluster' in Unit 5, mentioned above, the teacher might choose to tackle the Focus on writing 2 and Grammar practice 1, or set them for homework. The reading texts, in particular, will need to be well spaced.

Summaries of the contents of each unit are given in this book so that the teacher can plan the most appropriate sequence for the programme of work ahead. Note carefully where 'clusters' occur and follow the guidelines below:
—Always start with the Lead-in
—Keep 'clusters' intact
—Always finish with the Vocabulary review
The time needed to work through a unit will vary greatly according to the length of the unit, the interest generated by individual sections, the proportion which is set for homework, and so on. As a general rule, a unit will take a *minimum* of ten hours' classroom time and the whole course is likely to take 120–180 teaching hours.

A NOTE ON TEACHING APPROACH

The target level of the examination is, of course, very high, and it is one of the pitfalls of preparing students for Proficiency that they can easily be disheartened when presented with materials which seem only to confront them with their own ignorance. For this reason, it is extremely important to foster a sense of confidence from the beginning.

Two principles underpin this course.
— each learner has a unique contribution to make to the learning process, in terms of both language and experience.
— The greater the co-operation and mutual trust which is built up within the group, the more effective the learning will be.

The two principles are clearly underlined in the Communication activity for Unit 3 (The Desert Survival Problem) where the group consensus result is almost always more successful than the individual result.

The Lead-ins to each unit are a fundamental feature of the course. They serve the obvious purpose of awakening interest in the topic, practising skills necessary for the examination and extending topic vocabulary. More important, however, is their function of knitting students together into a co-operative team. They should be able to draw on their individual experience and linguistic resources and share them with each other in an enjoyable and non-threatening way. Most important of all, they should enter the next phase from a position of strength, not weakness.

NOTES ON INDIVIDUAL SECTIONS

Lead-in

The aim and importance of these sections has been described above. They represent a springboard to a unit and a way of bringing a class's resources, in terms of language and experience, to bear on a topic.

Lead-ins fall into two broad categories: The first group (Units 1, 3, 7, 8, 10) centres on pictures for description and discussion, and thus provides practice for the first phase of the Interview. The second group (Units 2, 4, 5, 6, 9) involves problem-solving, with students working in co-operation, and provides practice for the third phase of the Interview.

Reading texts

The 23 reading texts have been chosen to be as varied and interesting as possible. Students should always have a *reason* for reading. This may be to confirm or deny speculation about a subject (as in 'Why do we still dice with death?' – Text 1, Unit 5), to explore an interesting viewpoint (as in 'A medium of no importance' – Text 2, Unit 8), or to answer pre-set gist comprehension questions.

Thirteen of the texts have pre-questions in the student's book. For most of the others, optional pre-questions (and answers) have been suggested in the notes which follow. The intention has been to avoid a rigid formula and to allow the teacher freedom to tackle each unit as he/she pleases.

The vocabulary matching exercises are designed to encourage students to make logical deductions about the meanings of unknown words.
Note: For both the vocabulary matching and the multiple choice questions, it is extremely valuable if students are given time to compare and discuss their answers with one another before the correct answers are supplied.

It is assumed that teachers will include a more detailed question phase which will also highlight key vocabulary. This phase may precede or follow the multiple choice questions, as appropriate.

Details of the particular vocabulary items from a text which are included in the Vocabulary review section have been given to ensure that these items get adequate (but not undue) attention.

In Unit 1, the exercises for Text 1 have separate headings, and dotted lines indicate the approximate length of answer required for the questions on Text 2. These act as a guide for the tasks which appear in all subsequent units.

Focus on grammar

The grammar coverage is not, of course, comprehensive. (A tall order at this level!) I have tried, however, to ensure that the most important areas are covered in these sections. Study Boxes and Language Checks provide additional sources of information (see below). To supplement this area of work, a Proficiency level grammar reference such as *Grammar in Context* (Gethin, Collins), which incorporates extensive exercises and study lists, would be invaluable.

Study Boxes

There are either one or two Study Boxes in each unit and these provide handy reference sections on aspects of writing, grammar or vocabulary. Areas covered include letter and summary writing, phrasal verbs and easily confusable words such as *prevent* and *avoid*. Regular quick revision tests on Study Box material are recommended as a way of encouraging students to make active use of these sections.

Language checks

These represent 'do-it-yourself' Study Boxes. The students are invited to first test their accuracy with regard to an aspect of grammar or vocabulary and then, having checked the answers with the teacher or in a dictionary, to provide a reference list which will serve as a reference and revision aid for the future. Areas covered include dependent prepositions and aspects of vocabulary and word building.

These tasks can usually be done very productively in pairs and work well as 'warmer' activities at the start of a lesson. As with the Study Boxes, regular quick revision tests encourage students to use the Language Check material effectively.

Focus on writing

There is a wide range of descriptive and discursive topics in a variety of formats, including letters and reports.

Fairly detailed guidelines are given, particularly in the early units and it is advisable that these are discussed fully in class, and that students are given the opportunity for guided planning, on an individual or group basis, before the writing stage.

Note: useful additional reference material on letter and summary writing is given in two Study Boxes (see index) and students should be reminded to refer to them as necessary throughout the course.

Focus on listening

There are twelve listening texts included in Units 1 to 10 and these are recorded on an accompanying course cassette, while the tapescripts are reproduced at the end of this book.

The texts are generally longer than those given in the examination (where candidates usually hear three short extracts) and also involve a larger number of tasks. This is to allow for more extensive listening, which is appropriate at this level, and to provide a fuller context and more interesting material for classroom exploitation.

Always allow time for students to read the instructions and/or questions before they listen, and check that these are understood. Each text should normally be played through twice, without pauses. If students have particular difficulty after one hearing, pauses can be introduced but discourage reliance on this practice.

The follow-up should aim to go beyond merely checking answers; it should highlight useful vocabulary and structure and can also provide pronunciation practice or lead to discussion.

Note: eight additional listening texts are included in the Exam Practice section at the end of the book.

Focus on register

This feature practises the skills required for the third passage of the Reading Comprehension paper, in which the candidate is required to recognise form, register and intention, and also to be able to select and synthesise information from a variety of sources.

Communication activity

The purpose of these activities is not only to prepare for the third phase of the interview, but also to contribute very positively to the learning process. Teaching and learning at this level have a tendency to become rather cerebral, and these activities provide an opportunity for students to interact in pairs or groups, using language in a freer, more relaxed and more creative way.

The activities fall into two broad categories: the first (Units 1, 4, 6, 7, 9) involving an information gap of some kind, and the second (Units 2, 3, 4.2, 5, 8, 10) involving tasks in which the students co-operate to solve a problem, or reach agreement.

The teacher's notes on the individual sections are divided into three sections: preparation, pair work or role play, and feedback. The preparation stage sometimes involves preliminary discussion groups and the interaction in these is quite as important as that in

the following stage. Provided the preparation has been successful, students should be able to operate without any intervention on the teacher's part during the next stage, although he/she should be available, as a resource, to be called on by pairs who come across a problem.

It is most important that both students and teachers should recognise this change in the teacher's role and that it should be reflected both in the seating arrangements (as suggested in the notes) and in the teacher's position on the periphery. This is obviously not the time for heavy-handed correction!

All the activities work best if students are used to working together as a routine practice. Both the student's book and the teacher's notes give ample opportunity for this.

Among the many advantages which emerge from this type of work are the widely differing and imaginative results which pairs produce if left to work things out on their own, and the way in which the shyer and/or weaker students can often display unexpected talents.

Vocabulary practice

The Review exercises have 20–25 multiple choice questions in which the keys (correct answers) are always vocabulary items already met in one of the sections of the unit. *Note:* the sources of items are given in these notes so that students can be reminded of the original context.

In addition, there are five exercises on phrasal verbs and various other vocabulary exercises which relate to texts in the unit.

Grammar practice

Each unit has a cloze exercise on a theme related to the general topic and one other exercise in the examination format. These are suitable for homework.

Exam practice

This section provides additional practice material for Papers 4 (Listening Comprehension) and 5 (Interview) of the examination. Depending on the length and intensity of the course and the ability of the students, the material can either be reserved for intensive pre-exam preparation, or introduced at an earlier stage to give students the experience of examination tasks and familiarise them with procedures.

Listening

There are eight listening texts, the majority of which are authentic, and these are linked to topics in the book. The material is recorded on the accompanying Exam Practice cassette and the tapescripts are reproduced at the end of this book.

In most cases, the full conversation or interview is divided into two or more sections with a variety of question types. In each case, a brief introduction to interest and motivate students is recommended. In general, it is best to follow normal exam procedures by replaying each section before moving on to the next. Unless students seem to be experiencing particular difficulty, it is probably best not to check answers until the whole recording has been heard.

The eight listening texts in this section can either be reserved for intensive pre-exam practice, or introduced at an earlier stage to give students the experience of examination procedures.

Interview

There are six complete interview 'packages' and these also relate to topics in the book. Each package consists of three sections as in the examination and, for exam practice purposes, it is a good idea for students to have experience of working through a complete package on some occasions.

Sue O'Connell
Bristol, September '88

UNIT NOTES AND KEY
UNIT 1 Homes

▶Summary of contents

Note: In this and all the other contents lists, related sections are indicated in square brackets.

▶Lead-in (p. 4)

The three illustrations provide an opportunity to practise the detailed description required in the first part of the Interview in the Proficiency examination. Emphasize the *range* of vocabulary required at this level and the benefit of systematic vocabulary-building.

Architectural and other features which might usefully be included are:

tiled wooden/timber corrugated iron	roof	bay dormer	window
drainpipe gutter waterbutt	veranda(h) vs balcony porch	drive(way) path	
lawn shrub hedge flower bed	window sill shutters		

Descriptive terms

1 hut/cabin/shed; ramshackle; tumbledown; dilapidated; shabby; makeshift etc.

2 ranch-style; single–storey; rambling; landscaped etc.

3 detached; two-storey; substantial; neat/trim/orderly/well kept; suburban etc.

Encourage students to describe their own houses (or a typical house in their country) in some detail, and to account for differences in terms of climate, available building materials, life styles and density of population.

Other topics for discussion

Is it more usual in the students' countries to rent a house, or to have one built? How is money obtained for buying a dwelling? Do married couples find a place of their own or move in with in-laws (and what problems can this cause)? How is a new house or flat furnished (with second-hand items, bought or donated, or with brand new furniture)? etc.

▶Text 1 (p. 5)

Suggested lead-in

Ask students to suggest ways in which holiday accommodation can cost nothing (eg staying with friends; borrowing a holiday cottage or flat; camping; working in a hotel etc.) and exploit any experience students have had of these arrangements.

Introduce the idea of home-swapping, if it hasn't been suggested, and discuss briefly the advantages and potential problems.

Pre-questions (Reading for gist) – suggested answers

1 To match suitable families and arrange introductions with a view to their swapping homes for a holiday.

2 It issues questionnaires which applicants fill in with details of their homes and family circumstances.

3 Yes it was. The writer experienced friendliness and hospitality from his hosts and their friends, explored the area and learnt a great deal about the Texan way of life.

Vocabulary matching (Extending your vocabulary)
Line numbers are given in brackets.

a lavish (42); **b** sizeable (46); **c** sparse (60); **d** enclave (62); **e** bonhomie (64); **f** odd (65); **g** sports (84); **h** seething with (84); **i** enhanced (87); **j** delved into (89)

Multiple choice (Reading for detail)
Line numbers are given in brackets.

1 B (22–25); **2** D (16); **3** D (27, 34–36); **4** C (50–54); **5** A (100)

Vocabulary items included in Vocabulary review

an *enquiring* mind (1); set about (11); (in)compatible (12); lavish (42); sparse(ly) (60); the odd. . . (65); sheer (81)

►Focus on writing 1 (p. 6)

1 Revise vocabulary from the Lead-in and extend to cover other features such as: **building materials** eg stone, timber, brick, concrete, marble, plaster, etc.
   size eg sizeable, spacious, roomy, cosy, compact, cramped, etc.
   layout eg The lounge *opens off* the hall; The sitting room *opens on to* the garden; The bedroom *overlooks/looks on to* the garden; The bedroom is *up two flights* of stairs; The kitchen *adjoins* the dining room, etc.

2 Discuss the layout and structure of the letter (introduction, middle and conclusion), together with the main points for inclusion and their order of priority.

►Text 2 (p. 7)

Suggested lead-in

A striking picture of a desolate tower block would be ideal but a blackboard sketch would also serve as a focus for a preliminary discussion on the problems of high-rise living. Students can work in pairs to list difficulties and dangers. Ask them about personal experience of the subject or cases they may have read or heard about and exploit the information they give.

Possible pre-questions

1 What are the main problems faced by the remaining tenants of Towerhill?
2 What is the local council's attitude towards the tenants?
3 What action is the council considering taking to solve the problem?

Suggested answers

1 They have to put up with damp and mould which are a health risk and make it impossible to use some rooms – leading to overcrowding; they feel isolated and afraid; they are surrounded by rubbish which is a danger to children and at risk from gas explosions and fires; water leaks make electric fittings hazardous and can lead to flooding.

2 The council seems to despise the tenants and regard them as the cause of the problems.

3 The council is considering the possibility of demolishing the flats.

Vocabulary matching
Line numbers are given in brackets.

a ghastliest (13); **b** folly (13); **c** recriminations (18); **d** charred (33); **e** fragments (36); **f** looted (39); **g** devoured (39); **h** ripped (47); **i** evacuated (55); **j** dud (57); **k** shortcomings (71); **l** shambles (89); **m** sanction (109)

Suggested answers to questions

1 They cost a great deal to build and are now virtually uninhabitable.

2 They were deserted, damaged by fire, strewn with debris, have suffered from looting and had an eerie atmosphere.

3 By boarding up the empty flats, clearing up the debris, repairing serious water and gas leaks, treating the mould and by ensuring frequent police patrols.

4 'the scum of the earth' 'the butt end of the borough'.

5 A person who inspires and encourages others to act by his energy, determination, personality, ideas etc.

6 In order to find out if/prove that the design of the buildings had been faulty from the start.

7 He wanted to identify the defects in the structure more accurately.

8 Because one flat's bedroom was next to another's living room, causing disturbance, and because the flats were on two levels.

9 He argues that the tenants are uncooperative and, in fact, destroy what the council repairs.

10 The physical struggle of demolishing the strongly-built flats and the struggle to obtain the money necessary for demolition.

Vocabulary items included in Vocabulary review

derelict (12); mould(y) (24); overflow *with* (35); loot(ing) (39); evacuate (55); commission (63); report on (64); access (69); pinpoint (71); blame. . . on (91); pay. . . off (107); incur (107); demolition (109)

►Focus on writing 2 (p. 9)

Marks should be given for appropriate structure, style, expression and tone, and for inclusion of the following points:
difficulties: damp mould; unusable rooms; overcrowding; anxiety.
dangers: debris (risk of accidents to children); fires; gas explosions; flooding; water leaks; health risks.
action: short term – remove rubbish; board up empty flats; provide police surveillance; attend to gas/water leaks; stop removing window frames. Long term – rehouse tenants.

►Communication activity (p. 11)

Allow about 40 minutes for this activity.

Preparation

1 Introduce the role play by asking how people go about finding a new home and what factors they take into consideration. Exploit any experience students may have of house hunting. Check the term 'estate agent'.

2 Pair the students off and allot roles. Role B is probably best suited to the more confident speakers. Students read through the role play notes.

3 After a few minutes, all those with Role A form a group to discuss their task and the kinds of questions they should ask to elicit the information they need. For example, 'Whereabouts is it, exactly?' or 'How far is it from the centre?' *not* 'Is it situated centrally?'

4 The Role B group discuss their task and any problems of vocabulary.

5 Visit each group to make sure they fully understand the material and the task before beginning the role play.

Role play

1 The most suitable arrangement for this activity is for students to sit facing each other, one on each side of a desk or table.

2 Once the role play has started, monitor unobtrusively and be available to help any pairs who have a problem. Check particularly that Role B students are interpreting their material creatively – they should not simply read out the information or mention drawbacks freely, but use their imagination and try to persuade effectively.

3 As soon as one or two pairs have reached a decision, encourage the others to do the same.

Feedback

Check on the decisions which have been taken (there should be a good variety) and ask pairs to report back on their negotiations, particularly on how persuasive the estate agents have been. Ask what language they felt they lacked and briefly practise relevant language items.

▶Focus on register (p. 12)

The task is best set without introduction, but the checking phase can be exploited as suggested below.
1 B; **2** C; **3** A; **4** D; **5** B; **6** B; **7** D
Students should (a) identify the language function of each extract; (b) suggest where it might have been taken from; (c) describe any characteristic features of style.

The extracts

A *Instructions;* a family magazine/government pamphlet etc dealing with energy saving in the home; imperatives (Cover, Do, Draught-proof, leave).

B *Description of process;* a school text book/technical magazine etc describing how a cental heating system works; passive voice (hot water *is pumped*, cooler water *is returned*).

C *Persuasive description;* an advertisement for new houses in a newspaper or magazine; persuasive adjectives and adverbs, giving an attractive but rather vague image (individually designed, best quality, ample, lots of, much more).

D *Narrative/Description;* from a novel or short story; adjectives used to create a picture in the reader's mind (large, old, stone), especially the more figurative ones (a dignified distance).

▶Language check (p. 12)

Dependent Prepositions 1: Verb + Preposition

apply **for**	depend **on**
approve **of**	differ **from**
believe **in**	insist **on**
blame *something* **on** *somebody*	mistake *somebody* **for** *someone else*
blame *somebody* **for** *something*	overflow **with**
complain **to** *somebody* **about** *something*	regard *somebody/something* **as**
	succeed **in**
cover *something* **with** *something else*	suffer **from**
	take advantage **of**

▶Focus on grammar (p. 13)

2 Present Continuous/Progressive; **3** Past Simple; **4** Present Perfect; **5** Past Perfect; **6** Future Simple

Main uses of the passive voice

Students will absorb this information better if they are actively involved.

1 Ask students to give other examples of their own.

2 Ask where the notices would be seen and who they would be addressed to.

3 Students could briefly describe the journey of a letter in the same way.

4 Ask who the writer might be in each example.

Exercise

1 has been redecorated

2 were sent

3 was completed; is (has been) equipped

4 has been given; is now being sought

5 are invited; will be given

6 was being repaired/hadn't been repaired; was given

7 has been received/is received; will be processed; will be sent

8 had been imprisoned; were released

9 is spoken; is being overtaken

10 has been inspected; has been found; will be delivered

▶Focus on writing 3 (p. 14)

Suggested answer

Coffee beans are taken from a skin bag and placed in an iron ladle which is held over a fire. The beans are stirred with a rod to ensure that they are roasted evenly all over. Next they are emptied into a cooling dish and allowed to cool. Later they are transferred to a mortar and ground with a pestle. Meanwhile, water is poured into a large coffee pot and heated over the fire. The ground coffee is then added to the water in the coffee pot and the pot is again heated over the fire. Next, a few cardamom seeds are ground in the mortar and emptied into a smaller coffee pot. The contents of the large coffee pot are poured into the smaller one and the mixture is then transferred to a third smaller pot. Finally the coffee is poured from the smallest coffee pot into a cup.

▶Focus on listening (p. 15)

The photograph provides an opportunity for more practice in describing buildings. In this case, the multi-storey structure and ornate facade with arched windows contrast strikingly with previous pictures. Students may speculate on the building materials, number of occupants, and the location, for example, of the kitchen and main room for entertaining guests. The recorded talk supplies this information.

Give students time to study the two plans and check that they see the relationship between them before beginning the task.

Room/use	Letter
Kitchen	C
Living Room	O
Animal Stalls	D
Laundry	E
Mafraj	N
Lobby	B ← given
Entrance Hall	A
Grain Store	K
Wardrobe	J
Bathroom	F
Well	G
Diwan	H
Loading	L ← given
Grinding	M

Lexis

whitewashed; flanking; flights (of stairs); landings; arduous; lobby; in seclusion

►Vocabulary practice (p. 16)

Review

Text and line numbers are given in brackets.

1 B (1.60)	**6 D** (1.81)	**11 A** (1.65)	**16 A** (2.24)
2 C (2.69)	**7 C** (1.1)	**12 D** (2.107)	**17 D** (2.64)
3 A (2.71)	**8 B** (2.55)	**13 B** (2.12)	**18 B** (2.35)
4 C (1.42)	**9 B** (2.107)	**14 C** (2.91)	**19 D** (2.39)
5 D (1.11)	**10 C** (2.109)	**15 B** (1.12)	**20 C** (2.63)

Words describing the movement of liquids (p.17)

1 dripping; **2** pelting; **3** gurgling; **4** pour; **5** splash; **6** lapping;
7 flows; **8** gushing; **9** seeped; **10** trickling

Grammar practice (p. 18)

1 (1) forward; (2) number; (3) have; (4) may/might/could;
(5) meet/fulfil/satisfy; (6) occupation/activity; (7) grow/cultivate;
(8) consideration/account; (9) that; (10) spent; (11) likely/
expected/bound/sure; (12) so; (13) for; (14) built/located/
situated; (15) best (*not* most); (16) of; (17) present; (18) in/by

2 *a* The house was too badly damaged to be repaired.
  b 'You can hardly expect me to agree to/grant your request.'
  c Imagine my exasperation. . ./Imagine how exasperated I
    was/felt. . .
  d It will take you at least twenty minutes to reach the station.
  e I had my car resprayed at the garage last Saturday.
  f They urged me not/never to give up hope.
  g How often does your goldfish need/have to be fed?
  h She may well have been delayed.
  i None of the protesters was prosecuted.
  j It was not until next day that I heard the news.

UNIT **2 Work**

►Summary of contents

►Lead-in (p. 19)

1 If students work in pairs to perform this simple task, a great deal of discussion can be generated and the results can be unexpected and imaginative! In the feedback, there's obviously scope for the revision and extension of topic vocabulary.

2a Addressing the class as a whole involves quite a lot of risk for the individual student and the task therefore needs careful handling if it is not to result in an embarrassed (and embarrassing) silence. Give students about $1\frac{1}{2}$ minutes to concentrate on a particular memory and ask them to recall how old they were, why the job was so bad and exactly how they felt. The best springboard is for the teacher to tell his/her own entertaining 'horror story' first and then to invite other experiences. Accept as many as are offered but don't press unwilling students. These very real experiences can be most revealing and can help in the process by which the class bonds together as a group.

2b Collate ideas on the board, supplying vocabulary as necessary.

What adds up to job satisfaction?

Rather than checking understanding of the various points, or discussing them beforehand (with the teacher's interpretation perhaps influencing results), it's better to limit the introduction to an explanation of the *task*; ie numbering each point in order of importance. Pairs should then discuss the interpretation of any points that are unclear (eg Security) and call for help if they need it.

The teacher should, in any case, circulate so as to be easily accessible and in order to note interestingly contrasting priorities which can be discussed during the feedback. The feedback itself needs a light touch if it isn't to become long, drawn-out and repetitive.

►Text 1 (p. 20)

Pre-questions

1 In a factory as an apprentice.
2 That it was very undemanding.
3 The job with the Civil Service. Because it was boring.
4 The job with the builder's merchants.

Vocabulary matching

Line references are given in brackets.
a holed up (21); **b** snug (21); **c** wore off (21/22); **d** stagnant (22); **e** menial (23); **f** penetrated (26); **g** culminate (27); **h** fastness (28); **i** amiable (31); **j** contempt (31); **k** asserted (32); **l** malice (33); **m** undertow (39); **n** petty (40)

Multiple choice

Line references are given in brackets.
1 A (5); 2 B (15–17); 3 B (22); 4 D (36–37); 5 C (42–44)

Vocabulary items included in Vocabulary review

in awe of (5); strike as (18); culminate in (27); assert (32); redeem/redeeming (42); overwhelm (46).

►Focus on writing 1 (p. 22)

The introduction to this task emphasises the importance of planning an essay in note form and sets a simple illustrative task. Poor organisation of ideas resulting from lack of planning is a common failing in Proficiency composition work and good habits should be instilled from the start and regularly reinforced. It's a good idea to make a regular practice of asking students to hand in their notes with their essays.

►Text 2 (p. 23)

Suggested lead-in

Discuss: the concept of (sexual) equality at work and how far students agree with the principle; whether there are jobs which are intrinsically unsuitable for women; whether there are jobs where the sexes perform unequally (eg heavy lifting); the situation in students' own countries; any recent 'breakthroughs' the students have heard of (eg women pilots or women fighting fires); men in women's roles (eg 'househusbands') etc.

Pre-questions

Possible answers

1 (for women) higher pay; scope for ambitiousness; possibility of gaining further qualifications and promotion; (for men) protection against the use of women as cheap labour.

2 women's own poor self-images and their lack of assertiveness; the employers' trick of downgrading women's work so that unequal rates of pay persist.

Suggested answers to questions

1 The barrier separating those jobs traditionally associated with women from the rest of employment; a barrier which it was extremely difficult for women to pass.

2 They had accepted their menial roles and believed themselves incapable of coping with more challenging work.

3 They have created new paths in difficult territory, like pioneers, and led the way for others to follow.

4 It was a job traditionally thought of as unsuitable for women.

5 Because schools tend to reflect the established views of society.

6 In terms of recognised qualifications/certificates etc.

7 Because women's work was then downgraded by employers and they continued to earn less than men.

8 She now has the potential for promotion or for moving to another job.

9 That what they say won't make a good impression.

10 assertiveness; self-confidence; competitiveness.

11 Overcoming negative feminine attitudes/Adopting more masculine attitudes.

12 It is natural/instinctive.

13 Give marks for a well-expressed paragraph which includes the following points: menial roles/subservience to men; lack of career structure/prospect of promotion; lack of opportunity to move to other jobs; low pay; lack of opportunities to undergo training in order to gain formal qualifications; undervaluing of women's jobs and skills.

Vocabulary items included in Vocabulary review

to grasp (12); and the like (31–32); resist (39); take up (41–42); come into force (76); come over as (100); to counter (111); wary (113); capacity (123).

►Focus on grammar 1 (p. 25)

It provides useful consolidation if students suggest alternative examples to illustrate the main uses of the tense.

Exercise 1

1 see – view/watch (as eg)
    – visit/meet (as eg)
  hold – contain
    – keep
  depend – rely on
      – be influenced by
  apply – make an application
    – be relevant
  fit – be the right size
    – install
  look – appear
    – search

2 *Note:* contracted forms are also acceptable.

a has only applied
b have never looked
c has been seeing
d have been depending
e has been applying
f has held
g have seen
h have been fitting
i has depended
j have been looking
k have been holding
l have fitted

Exercise 2

Note: The original text used the Present Simple to recount Sister Browne's various activities during the day. The Present Continuous could also be used and both possibilities are given in the answers below. The use of one or the other should, however, be consistent.

1	has been working/has worked	16	is doing
2	directs	17	enters
3	have been assigned/ are assigned	18	switches
4	has been calculated	19	has arrived
5	move	20	wear
6	qualified	21	has got used to
7	has worked	22	notices
8	done	23	has/is having
9	exceeds	24	has recently been admitted
10	has just ended	25	have lived/have been living
11	listens/is listening	26	jokes/is joking
12	explains/is explaining	27	be taken
13	chats/is chatting	28	specialises
14	has been waiting	29	has banned
15	has just been interrupted	30	has finished
		31	snatches/is snatching

▶Communication activity (p. 28)

Allow 20–25 minutes for each activity. *Note:* the two activities can be used on separate occasions.

Part 1

Suggested preparation

1 Use magazine pictures, or the students themselves, to practise describing clothes, and to revise and extend topic vocabulary eg 2-piece/3-piece/pin-striped suit; waistcoat; sports jacket; evening dress; V-neck/polo-neck/turtle-neck sweater; jeans, trousers, slacks; flat/high-heeled shoes, boots, plimsolls, trainers; tapering/flared; smart/scruffy/shabby; baggy/tight-fitting, etc.

2 Discuss, briefly, students' own attitudes to clothes: how important they are; whether they affect one's mood; quality versus quantity; whether they would be prepared to wear formal clothes for a particular job; how far they judge people by their clothes.

Pair work

Point out that each pair *must* come to an agreement on a response to each statement. They should discuss each one so that they can give reasons for their answer. If there is a difference of opinion they should try to persuade each other. 'Sloppy' (careless/untidy) can be pre-taught.

Feedback

Afterwards, discuss the class's results and reasons in relation to the results of the *Which?* survey.

Part 2

1 Check comprehension of the jobs listed before pair-work begins. (*Note:* 'researcher' here refers to someone doing research for TV or radio programmes.) During pairwork, help out with any problem vocabulary if asked (eg battered, sober, jazzy).

2 Again, discuss results and reasons in relation to the results of the *Which?* survey. Draw students' attention to interesting comments, eg 'acceptable for behind-the-scenes staff' (number 6).

▶Focus on grammar 2 (p. 30)

Exercise 1

a stopped; *b* consider it carefully; *c* discussed; *d* investigating; *e* abandon, cancel; *f* arrived; *g* extinguish; *h* learn, manage; *i* inventing; *j* declined

Exercise 2

a; e; g; h; i

Exercise 3

	in	down	off	on	out	up
carry			x	x	x	
cut		x	x		x	x
fill	x				x	x
give	x		x		x	x
hand	x	x			x	
make			x		x	x
pay	x		x		x	x
turn	x	x	x	x	x	x

Notes:

carry off – gain/obtain (eg prizes)
carry on – continue
carry out – execute
cut down – fell (a tree)
cut off – disconnect
fill in }
fill out } complete (eg a form)
give in – yield/surrender
give off – emit (eg a smell)
give out – distribute
give up – stop

hand down – pass on, as a tradition
make off – escape
make out – distinguish
make up – invent
pay in – deposit
pay off – repay a debt
turn in – go to bed
turn down – reject
turn out – produce (eg industrial items)
turn up – arrive

Many of the above phrasal verbs also have other meanings. For detailed information about the meaning and use of phrasal verbs, see the *Dictionary of Phrasal Verbs* (Collins ELT).

Further practice

Students choose 10 phrasal verbs with which they are unfamiliar, check their meanings and write sentences to illustrate them.

▶Language check (p. 31)

Make vs Do
Make *a suggestion, an offer, a profit, an excuse, an attempt, money, fun of, sure, a choice, a decision, room for, the best of, use of, a complaint, a mistake, certain, a journey, an effort, an arrangement, an enquiry, the most of, a discovery, war.*

Do *an examination, a favour, homework, damage, one's best, harm, an exercise, one's duty, business, good, housework, work.*

▶Focus on listening (p. 32)

```
INTERVIEW REPORT FORM
1  Job title: .Ground Hostess / Reception Staff......
2  Name of applicant: .Rosemary Jones..........
3  Address: .12 Regent Street..   permanent          temporary
   ...........Stanmore..........   accommodation ☐   accommodation ☑
   ...........Middlesex.........
4  Age: under 20 ☐   20–24 ☑   25–30 ☐   over 30 ☐
5  Educational qualifications:
   CSE ☐      O Level ☐    A Level ☑    degree ☐
   details of subjects ...............................
6  Foreign languages spoken:
                          Standard
              Fluent   Very good   Good    Fair
   a  French     ☐        ☐         ☐      ☑
   b  Spanish    ☑        ☐         ☐      ☐
   c  German     ☐        ☐         ☐      ☑
7  Work experience:
   industrial ☐     commercial ☐     retail ☑
   casual labour ☐  voluntary ☑      other ☑
   eg building site
   details: .helper in old people's home........
8  General health and fitness:
   Excellent ☑     Good ☐     Fair ☐     Poor ☐
9  Hobbies:
   Sport ☑      Music ☐      Theatre/Cinema ☑
   Handicrafts ☐   Other ☑
   eg sewing
10 Personality:
   shy/nervous ☐     cold/distant ☐    relaxed/friendly ☑
   too casual/informal ☐   overconfident ☐
11 Details of availability: .not Friday mornings......
12 Starting salary offered: £ .115. (for 30 hours)
```

▶Focus on register (p. 33)

1 A (corner stone); 2 D; 3 C (a Board appointment); 4 D;
5 B

Vocabulary items included in Vocabulary review
B coupled with; under pressure

▶Vocabulary practice (p. 34)

Review

Text and line numbers are given in brackets. RB = Register B etc.

1 B (Lead in)	7 A (2.31–32)	13 C (RB)	19 C (2.123)
2 D (1.5)	8 B (2.111)	14 D (RB)	20 A (1.32)
3 A (1.27)	9 C (2.41–42)	15 A	21 C (Listening)
4 B (1.42)	10 D (2.12)	(Listening)	22 A (1.29)
5 D (2.100)	11 B (2.122)	16 D (2.60)	23 D (1.18)
6 C (1.46)	12 A (2.39)	17 C (2.113)	24 B (Listening)
		18 B (2.76)	25 C (2.125)

Phrasal verbs: TAKE

1 took up; 2 take it in; 3 taken over; 4 takes off; 5 taken up;
6 take after; 7 take you in; 8 take on; 9 took to; 10 take
you up; 11 take out; 12 taken in

▶Grammar practice (p. 37)

1 (1) in; (2) than; (3) catch; (4) source/example; (5) undergo;
(6) spend; (7) considered/calculated/estimated/wondered/
thought; (8) up; (9) aspects/parts/sides; (10) have; (11)
away; (12) full; (13) typing; (14) to; (15) amount

2 *a He struck me as a* highly efficient manager.
  b I took it for granted that you would ask me for a reference.
  c At first *I was* a bit *in awe of* the new computer.
  d Shouldn't you *cut down (on)* your smoking/your consumption
    of cigarettes/the (number of) cigarettes you smoke?
    or Shouldn't you *cut down on* cigarettes?
  e You have *the option of taking* early retirement.
  f I only called the police *as a last resort.*
  g Women in this factory work *on the same terms* as men.
  h However hard you (may) try, you won't succeed.

Erdan
Kizginkaya

UNIT 3 Tourist or Traveller?

►Summary of contents

►Lead-in (p. 38)

Pictures

The four pictures with their accompanying questions provide practice for the first part of the Interview in the Proficiency examination. Encourage students to:
1 use the language of speculation.
    eg It *seems* to be a tropical country, maybe in Africa.
        They *might/could/well* be American tourists.
        It *looks as if* they are scientists or explorers.
        There's a ship in the background which *looks like* a large liner.

2 exploit the details in the pictures to the full, mentioning, for example, features of appearance, expression, atmosphere and surroundings.

3 *stretch* their vocabulary so that they use precise rather than general terms. Teach relevant vocabulary, eg baggy trousers, thick undergrowth.

Buzz groups

1 Give groups a time limit (eg 3–5 minutes) and explain that they are to list as many differences as possible in the time, without too much discussion.

2 Collate the various points on the board under the two headings and discuss the issues they raise.

General discussion points

These three questions preview topics in the two texts in this unit and should be discussed as fully as possible.

Encourage students to talk from personal experience wherever possible.

►Text 1 (p. 39)

Note: Paul Theroux is an American writer who made a journey by train from his home town of Medford in the USA to Patagonia in the far south of South America. This passage is an extract from the book he wrote about his experiences.

Pre-question Suggested answer
The writer prefers to travel alone, for self discovery and contemplation which he sees as essential to his writing.

Multiple choice

1 C (2–3); **2** D (8); **3** C (10–12); **4** A (8–10); **5** D (1, 19, 27–29)

Vocabulary items included in Vocabulary review

unencumbered (2); shatter (5); drive to (15); self-conscious (17); abject (21); refute (23); crave (27)

►Focus on grammar 1 (p. 40)

Exercise 1

a Rarely do you see. . .
b Seldom have we met. . .
c Under no circumstances should you. . .
d At no time did I leave. . .
e Not until the police came would they confess. . .
f Nobody could she rely on but him.
g Nowhere could the keys be found.
h Not only did we run. . .

►Language check (p.41)

Dependent Prepositions 2: Preposition + Noun

on/for sale	**in** doubt
under cover of	**on** the left
to be **of** interest	**in** the left-hand corner
in contrast to	**at** the left-hand end
on a journey/voyage/trip	**in** danger of (+ing)
at no extra charge	**with** the intention of (+ing)
in aid of	to be **of** the opinion that
with the aid of	**in** the habit of (+ing)

►Text 2 (p. 42)

Possible pre-questions

1 What kind of amateur photography is referred to in the text?
2 What is the writer's opinion of the activity?
3 Give some of her reasons.

Answers

1 Tourist's holiday photographs.
2 It serves no useful purpose.
3 Photography dominates the holiday experience; it makes tourists aggressive; it distorts reality etc.

Suggested answers to questions

1 'hordes', 'flood', 'infestation', 'myriad'

2 That they move in vast numbers (as locusts swarm) and are destructive (as locusts devastate the vegetation).

3 Because taking photographs seems to be the most important holiday activity and the camera seems to dictate how the holiday is organised.

4 They are regarded as strange, old-fashioned, and with less important reasons for being there.

5 That all the complicated adjustments are made with such care and solemnity that the process resembles a religious ceremony.

6 They grab/exact/demand/get as much as they can from people who seem to be exploiting them.

7 To provide evidence of where the tourist has been.

8 on the pretext of/while pretending to/while seeming to

9 That they diminish/reduce and make ordinary the wonderful sights they have seen.

10 They concentrate on the most attractive scenes and do not reflect reality.

11 They must appear to be free from tourists.

12 Because they don't fit the idealised impression of the country which the tourist wants to convey.

13 By manipulating the camera to cut out the less romantic aspects of the scene and so create an unrealistic image.

14 Give marks for a well-expressed paragraph including the following points: photography more important than observation; self-important/intolerance of the photographer; trivial, egocentric purpose; lack of concern with reality of country; creation of false, idealised images.

Vocabulary items included in Vocabulary review

infest/infestation (5); wrench (29); shrink (69); obliterate (121)

▶ Focus on grammar 2 (p. 44)

Exercise 1

a provided that; run (1b)
b Without; would/will be (2/1b)
c on condition that; published (2)
d Supposing; will/would you be able (1b)
e Unless; will come (1b)
f As long as; won't (1b)
g in case; occur (1b)
h Given; will probably run (1b)

Exercise 2

Students should (a) underline the expressions introducing conditional clauses in each sentence, and (b) classify each sentence as Type 1a, 1b, or 2.

▶ Focus on writing (p. 46)

The two main pitfalls in tackling directed writing exercises are (a) failure to exploit the given information fully, and (b) failure to follow instructions. For example, a hasty reading of the instructions for this exercise could produce an irate letter to the hotel proprietor rather than the required one to the magazine editor. An error of this kind would probably cost the candidate all his/her marks for the question.

▶ Focus on listening 1 (p. 46)

Destination	Method(s) of travel	Number of days	Price range	Type of accommodation	Extra features
Malta	P	14	2	hotel	free car hire for 1 week
Venice	T	X	4	X	X
India	O/P	X	4	camping	free hire of camping equipment
Scotland	T	3	1	castle	children under 3 free
Ireland	O/S	X	1	farmhouse	children under 3 free

Lexis

an aversion to; gratuities; in a class of its own; intrepid; stamina; facilities[R]

[R]included in Vocabulary review

▶ Communication activity (p. 47)

Allow 45 minutes to one hour for this activity.

Preparation

Optional: Pre-teach selected items from those listed below under *Feedback.*

1 Make sure everyone has understood and absorbed the details of the situation and the problem. Check that students are following the correct procedure for the individual task.

2 Organise students into groups of 6–10 (8 is an ideal number) ensuring that there is at least one confident speaker in each group.

3 It is very important to *rearrange seating* for the group task: (a) to underline the student-centred nature of the activity, and (b) to facilitate informal discussion. Arrange chairs in a fairly small circle, or, if this is impossible, group chairs round desks or tables.

Group task

1 Stay quite separate from the group or groups and avoid the temptation to stage-manage at all costs. Any initial hesitance will quickly be overcome as long as groups are left to tackle the problem in their own way. It's quite a good idea to leave the room for the first 5 minutes, in fact. Any monitoring should be unobtrusive.

2 When the task is finished, refer students to the notes on scoring and help where necessary. Obviously only one (good mathematician) needs to calculate the group score.

Feedback

1 *Either* refer students to p. 196, which gives the expert ranking with brief reasons, and supply fuller information yourself from

the rationale below *or* give them the expert ranking and reasons orally.

2 Allow the group/s to comment on their experience of group co-operation and discuss the relevance of the activity to their language learning. Ask what language they felt they lacked and include a brief practice phase of relevant language items:

Agreeing: I (quite) agree with X.
I think X is absolutely right.
That's a good point.

Disagreeing: I'm not sure I agree with that.
I don't think that's quite true,
I think you may be mistaken.

Conceding: All right, I'll accept your argument.
Well, I'm prepared to go along with the rest.
You may be right, after all.

Initiating: In my opinion. . .
It seems to me that. . .
Wouldn't you agree that. . . ?

Consolidating: Do we all agree that. . . ?
So is everyone agreed that. . . ?

Co-ordinating: Let's vote on it, shall we?
What do *you* think, X?
I think someone else should have a chance to speak.

The Expert Alonzo W Pond is the desert survival expert who has contributed the basis for the item ranking. He is the former Chief of the Desert Branch of the Arctic, Desert, Tropic Information Centre of the US Air Force University at Maxwell Air Force Base.

During World War II, Mr Pond spent much of his time working with the Allied Forces in the Sahara on desert survival problems. While there and as a Chief of the Desert Branch, he encountered the countless survival cases which serve as a basis of the rationale for these rankings.

1 *Cosmetic mirror*
Of all the items the mirror is absolutely critical. It is the most powerful tool you have for communicating your presence. In sunlight a simple mirror can generate 5 to 7 million candle power of light. The reflected sunbeam can even be seen beyond the horizon. If you had no other items you would still have better than an 80 per cent chance of being spotted and picked up within the first 24 hours.

2 *One overcoat per person*
Once you have a communication system to tell people where you are, your next problem is to slow down dehydration. Forty per cent of the body moisture that is lost through dehydration is lost through respiration and perspiration. Moisture lost through respiration can be cut significantly by remaining calm. Moisture lost through perspiration can be cut by preventing the hot, dry air from circulating next to the skin. The top coats are the best means for doing this. Without them, survival time would be cut by at least a day.

3 *One litre of water per person*
You could probably survive three days with just the first two items. Although the litre of water would not significantly extend the survival time, it would help hold off the effects of dehydration. It would be best to drink the water as you become thirsty so that you remain as clear-headed as possible during the first day when important decisions have to be made and a shelter erected. Once dehydration begins it would be impossible to reverse it with the amount of water available in this situation. Therefore, rationing it would do no good at all.

4 *Torch*
The only quick, reliable night signalling device is the torch. With it and the mirror you have a 24 hour signalling capability. The reflector and lens could also be used during the day as an auxiliary signalling device or for starting a fire. The battery container could also be used for digging or as a water container in the distillation process (see plastic raincoat).

5 *Parachute*
The parachute can serve as both shelter and signalling device. Certain cactus could serve as the tent pole and the parachute ropes as tent ropes. Double or triple folding the parachute would give shade dark enough to reduce the temperature underneath it by as much as 20 per cent.

6 *Jack knife*
Although not as crucial as the first 5 items, the jack knife would be useful for rigging the shelter and for cutting up the very tough cactus for moisture. Its innumerable other uses gives it the high ranking.

7 *Plastic raincoat*
The difference in temperature produced by digging a hole and placing the raincoat over it will extract some moisture from pieces of cactus and produce condensation on the underside of the plastic. A cone shape can be formed by placing a small stone in the centre of the plastic, causing moisture to drip into the battery container of the torch which is buried in the centre of the hole.

8 *.45 calibre pistol*
By the end of the second day speech would be seriously impaired and you might be unable to walk. The pistol would then be useful as a sound signalling device and the bullets as a quick fire starter. There have been numerous cases of survivors going undetected because they couldn't make any loud sounds. The butt of the pistol might also be used as a hammer.

9 *A pair of sunglasses per person*
In the intense sunlight of the desert eye conditions similar to snow blindness could be serious problems especially by the second day. Handkerchiefs or bandages could be used to protect the eyes but sunglasses would be more comfortable.

10 *Bandage kit*
Because of the desert's low humidity, it is considered one of the healthiest places in the world. Owing to the fact that the blood thickens with dehydration, there is little danger from bleeding unless a vein is severed. The kit materials might be used as rope or for wrapping legs, ankles and head, including face – a further protection against dehydration and sunlight.

11 *Magnetic compass*
Apart from the possibility of using its reflective surfaces as an auxiliary signalling device, the compass is of little use. It could even be dangerous to have around once the effects of dehydration set in. It might encourage walking out.

12 *Sectional air map of the area*
Might be helpful for starting a fire or for one man to use as a head cover or eye shade. But essentially useless and perhaps dangerous as it too might encourage walking out.

13 *A Book entitled: 'Edible Animals of the Desert'*
The problem confronting the group is dehydration, not starvation. Any energy expended in hunting would be costly in terms of potential water loss. Desert animals, while plentiful, are seldom seen. They survive by lying as low as should the survivors. If the hunt was successful, the intake of protein would cause an increase in the amount of water used to process it. General rule of thumb: if you have lots of water, eat, otherwise don't consume anything.

14 *2 quarts of 180 proof vodka*

When severe alcoholism kills someone, they usually die of dehydration. Alcohol absorbs water. The vodka consumed could be lethal in this situation. Its presence could cause someone in a dehydrated state to increase his problem. It would be helpful for a fire or as a temporary coolant for the body. The bottle might also be useful. All in all the vodka represents more dangers than help.

15 *Bottle of salt tablets*

With dehydration and loss of water, blood salinity increases. Without lots of extra water the salt tablets would require body water to get rid of the increased salinity. The effect would be like drinking sea water.

▶Focus on register (p. 49)

1 C (1: horn-honking traffic jams; 2: fire sirens may wail all night)

2 D (Such enthusiastic self-indulgence is a vice I am more prone to in New York. . .)

3 A (2: it's one of the world's most exciting and beautiful cities/New York is the place where it's all happening; 3: a quality which is peculiar to New York itself.)

4 C (New York's menacing streets. . . fortunately do not approach their notoriety.)

5 C (Common sense and an alert eye. . . trouble will not find you.)

Vocabulary items included in Vocabulary review

A jostling; **B** shrug, dismiss, billow, deface; **C** prone to, shed, peculiar to; **D** on the *alert*, reckless, steer clear of, run-down

▶Focus on listening 2 (p. 51)

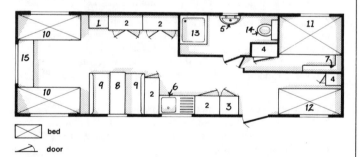

☒ bed

◿ door

Lexis

The room *sleeps* two; too much of a *squash*; roomy; bunk bed; the seat can *serve as* an extra bed; plumbed-in; a deposit *against* breakages, refundable

▶Vocabulary practice (p. 52)

Review

1 C (1.17)	**8** B (RB)	**14** C (RD)	**20** D (1.21)
2 D (1.5)	**9** A (RC)	**15** A (2.69)	**21** A (L1)
3 A (RA)	**10** B (2.29)	**16** B (2.5)	**22** B (RC)
4 D (RB)	**11** C (RB)	**17** B (1.27)	**23** D (RD)
5 D (RD)	**12** D (RB)	**18** A (1.15)	**24** C (RD)
6 C (2.121)	**13** B (RC)	**19** D (1.23)	**25** B (1.2)
7 C (Fog)			

R = Register; L = Listening; Fog = Focus on grammar

Words describing facial expression

1 frown (vb; n – wrinkle forehead expressing displeasure, worry, or concentration)

2 glared (vb; n – stare angrily)

3 beamed (vb; n – smile happily)

4 gaped (vb – stare open-mouthed in surprise)

5 grimaced (vb; n – ugly, twisted expression of disgust or pain)

6 pout (vb; n – push out lips in a sulky way)

7 smirked (vb; n – smile in a silly, self-satisfied way)

8 Leering (vb; n – look in an unpleasant, lecherous way)

9 grin (vb; n – smile broadly)

10 scowling (vb; n – look bad-tempered)

▶Grammar practice (p. 54)

1 (1) can/usually/often/sometimes/normally/ occasionally/ frequently; (2) myself; (3) set; (4) destination; (5) Although; (6) as; (7) gathered/gained/acquired/accumulated; (8) apply; (9) mind; (10) had; (11) involved; (12) whom; (13) familiar/ acquainted/those; (14) calm; (15) providing/supplying; (16) Needless; (17) evidence/proof; (18) Anyone; (19) deserves/ merits; (20) event

2 *a* Have you made/taken/come to

b I'm thinking

c could be lying/sunbathing on

d doesn't appeal

e Would you

f I (really) like/enjoy/love

I'm (really) fond of/keen on

g had told me/had mentioned that/had said so

h 's (has) been nobody

UNIT 4 Relationships

►Summary of contents

►Lead-in (p. 55)

Quiz

This activity can either be done individually and then answers compared, as suggested in the book, or it can be done by pairs. Either way, it should involve discussion.

1 Ask students to draw on their own experience, what they have read or heard or what they *guess* the situation to be. They *must* choose an answer for each question.

2 Invite a brief class discussion before giving answers or telling students to refer to page 197 (answer key). Compare the answers to questions 1 and 2 with the situation in the students' own countries.

What is a close friend?

Encourage students to add an extra definition of their own (eg someone who accepts me for what I am). If the class is mixed, tabulate the results under Male and Female headings on the board and see if there are any significant differences.

Vocabulary items included in Vocabulary review

relieve (1); given. . . (2) apart from. . . (2)

►Text 1 (p. 58)

Suggested lead-in

Elicit from students words for 'differences of opinion'. This can be done by giving the first letters of a number of words on the board (eg *argument, quarrel, row, dispute, disagreement, conflict, dissension*). You could perhaps teach *feud, squabble, tiff*.

Query the difference between an argument and a quarrel. Ask 'Do you argue or quarrel about politics?' but leave the question unresolved.

Vocabulary matching

a fractious (9); **b** siblings (9); **c** attrition (12);**d** pretext (21); **e** inclination (27); **f** sifting (29); **g** neophyte (36); **h** spouses (37); **i** stakes (39); **j** tenacious (45)

Multiple choice

1 D (26–30); **2** B (41–44); **3** C (10–13; 45–47); **4** A (66/67); **5** B (3–5; 6/7, 53)

Vocabulary items included in Vocabulary review

resources (1); capacity (3); pretext (21); by inclination (27); sift (29); fraud (30); be denied to (43); on one's hands (51); remorse (question 1)

►Text 2 (p. 60)

Suggested lead-in

1 Sketch a semi-detached house on the board and ask students to work in pairs and list potential problems which can arise between close neighbours (3–5 minutes).

2 Ask the pairs to report back. Write the problems on the board in three groups – those concerning noise, those concerning fumes and those concerning other disturbances. Ask students to suggest headings for the three groups. Alternatively, list problems randomly on the board and ask students to decide on three groups.

3 Ask for and exploit any personal experiences students have had of such problems. Ask too what action they would take if they were disturbed by, say, frequent noisy parties next door. Discuss possible results.

Possible pre-questions

1 Read the passage and note any problems not listed on the board.
2 How did Michael react when his neighbour disturbed him?
3 What two solutions does the law offer?

Answers

2 By trying to cause his neighbour even more annoyance in return.

3 An injunction (a court order to stop the nuisance) or damages in compensation for suffering.

Suggested answers to questions

1 They were very obliging and helpful.

2 They are forced to live in close proximity to one another. Normally one chooses who one wishes to be intimate with.

3 To limit topics of conversation to safe, neutral ones, like the weather.

4 A small opening in the defence system of trivial remarks/a slight departure from the general rule of exchanging only commonplace remarks (ie a more personal comment).

5 'sympathetic chats' aim to sort out a problem in a friendly, understanding way; 'face to face confrontation' is more aggressive and uses threats or ultimata rather than discussion.

6 The effect which hearing the terrible rows might have on the child.

7 The person who takes the most extreme course of action will succeed.

8 'a war of escalation'

9 To spoil his neighbours' enjoyment of their garden by causing dense smoke to blow over it.

10 It must be a plant which would have a harmful effect on his neighbour's garden.

11 The payment of money to make up for suffering caused.

12 That he was sympathetic towards her.

13 Give marks for a well-expressed paragraph including the following points: noise; musical instruments; arguments; electrical appliances; fumes; bonfires or car exhausts; other nuisance such as unsocial hobbies or boundary disputes.

Vocabulary items included in Vocabulary review

blight (10); insurance against (12); barricade (13); breach (17); the best part of (34); recourse to (39); onslaught (45); lethal (73); persist/persistent (81)

▶Focus on grammar (p. 62)

Exercise

a The car may/might/could have been sold
b if he could/might write
c you obviously won't/can't have heard
d The line can't have been engaged
  There could/may/might be
e He might/may/could have taken
f Where might/could I find
g if I might use
h People will/must have been looking
i You might/may not even have to
j She won't/can't have left

▶Focus on writing (p. 64)

It is extremely helpful to go through the notes on *preparation* and *planning* orally with the class. In particular, the four questions under *preparation* should be discussed as fully as possible, so that students have plenty of ideas to draw on.

▶Communication activity (p. 64)

Allow about 30 minutes for this activity.

Preparation

1 An oral introduction to the topic is essential. A simple approach would be to write the term 'Self-Assertion' on the board and ask students to speculate as to what it means. When the concept is understood, explain that Self-Assertion classes have become quite common in Britain and the United States in recent years and ask why classes for women seem to be particularly popular. Remind them of Cristina Stuart's comments in the last part of Text 2, Unit 2.

2 Ask students to read the notes on the three types of behaviour and check comprehension thoroughly. Practise saying the example statements in types 1 and 2 with appropriate stress and intonation.

3 A further example might be helpful before proceeding: You're travelling by train and trying to study for an exam. Someone keeps trying to engage you in conversation and you really don't want to talk to him/her. How would you react (a) *aggressively*? (eg Say 'Can't you be quiet and let me read!') (b) *non-assertively*? (Put down your book with a sigh and talk to him) (c) *assertively*? (Say: 'I don't want to be rude but I really do want to concentrate on my book.')

Discrimination exercise

1 Go through situation 1 and the example assessment. Practise appropriate stress and intonation.

2 Encourage pairs to try saying the various options in the way they interpret them.

3 Compare pairs' results with those given in the Key on p. 197. Discuss any differences of opinion and practise saying responses appropriately.

Practice situations

Draw students' attention to the instruction concerning the notes marked **A**. Tell them to read the notes for each situation very carefully before beginning each roleplay and to ask for help if anything is unclear. Monitor unobtrusively.

Feedback

Ask pairs to report back briefly on their success at self-assertion and counter-assertion. Allow them to compare notes if the information gap has not been fully bridged! A practice phase of relevant language items may be useful.

Vocabulary items included in Vocabulary review

Help (somebody) out

▶Focus on listening (p. 67)

1 B (neon strip lights overhead cast a glare/icy blasts from the door)

2 D (it's a great comfort to. . . come down here and have a chat with May and Burnie)

3 A

4 C (watching out for 12 year olds in case they flood the place)

5 A (Their customers respond by. . . pouring out their troubles like children)

6 B

Lexis

battered; buzzing with (activity); linger[R], faded[R]; a glare; protruding (handles); icy blasts; bed-bound; things get on top of you; strapping (men); darning

[R]included in Vocabulary review

▶Focus on writing 2 (p. 68)

As the subject is a very personal one, it does not lend itself to discussion beforehand. It is perhaps best to restrict preparation to the language of description; build, posture, facial features, expression, character, etc. A set of pictures illustrating some of these features would be an invaluable aid.

There is a danger that this kind of preparation, while a useful vocabulary building exercise in itself, could have a counter-productive effect on the eventual composition. Students may take the opportunity to practise as much of the new vocabulary as possible, producing wordy, unbalanced and rather lifeless accounts. To avoid this pitfall, draw students' attention to point 1a.

▶Focus on register (p. 68)

1 C; **2** D; **3** D; **4** B; **5** C

▶Language check (p. 69)

Dependent Prepositions 3: Adjective + preposition

capable **of**	ignorant **of**
compared **to/with**	keen **on**
contrary **to**	regardless **of**
convinced **of**	responsible **for**
deprived **of**	satisfied **with**
familiar **with**	subject **to**
fed up **with**	surprised **at/about**
guilty **of**	suspicious **of/about**

▶Vocabulary practice (p. 70)

Review

1 D (1.3)	**8 C** (1.q1)	**14 C** (2.34)	**20 C** (L)
2 C (1.21)	**9 A** (2.73)	**15 B** (L)	**21 D** (2.39)
3 A (2.10)	**10 B** (1.30)	**16 A** (2.81)	**22 A** (2.45)
4 D (2.17)	**11 D** (CA)	**17 A** (1.27)	**23 C** (Ld-I.1)
5 B (1.29)	**12 C** (1.43)	**18 C** (2.12)	**24 A** (Ld-I.2)
6 B (2.13)	**13 B** (1.1)	**19 D** (2.30)	**25 B** (Ld-I.2)
7 A (1.51)			

The adjective suffix '-some'

quarrelsome; troublesome; loathesome; irksome; awesome; meddlesome; wearisome; tiresome; fearsome.

argumentative; problematic; hateful; annoying; reverential; interfering; dreadful

a cumbersome; *b* wholesome; *c* burdensome

Verbs ending in '-ate'

a infuriate; **b** retaliate; **c** escalate; **d** compensate; **e** substantiate; **f** fluctuate; **g** gesticulate; **h** vacate; **i** manipulate; **j** fabricate

▶Grammar practice (p. 72)

1 (1) at; (2) far; (3) able; (4) unless; (5) close; (6) another; (7) these; (8) its; (9) fact; (10) develop; (11) infancy; (12) birth; (13) fed; (14) to; (15) kind/sort/type; (16) form; (17) other; (18) only; (19) control; (20) themselves/it

2 *a* having written the letter.
 b the fact that it rained torrentially all day/the torrential rain (all day)
 c had I recovered from bronchitis than I
 d is the Manager to be disturbed; must/should/the Manager be disturbed.
 e me of being a liar/of lying.
 f we hear from you in seven days,
 g is being relayed by satellite.
 h though/as he may seem,
 i your generous contribution,
 j he telephones, he wants to

UNIT 5 Health

▶Summary of contents

▶Lead-in (p. 73)

Possible preliminary activity

(books closed)

1 Ask students to write down *two* aspects of their lives which might be considered to have a positive effect on their health and *two* things which might be considered to have a negative effect. These might include eating and drinking habits, physical activity (or lack of it), stress and relaxation etc.

2 After two or three minutes ask for and discuss the various points. Discuss also students' attitudes towards health (is it an important consideration in their lives?), whether we are more health-conscious these days than we used to be, and whether we are *actually* healthier nowadays. The class could also consider the factors in modern life which have a negative effect on health.

Note: You will find it useful to make a note (for yourself) of the fitter and less fit members of the class (this will help with the Communication activity).

Pairwork

The students' basic task is to decide how dangerous a number of activities are (i.e. how likely they are to kill you over a 10-year period).

1 Go through the instructions, making sure they are fully understood and giving one or two hypothetical examples if necessary. Explain that each pair should discuss the different risks, using their personal experience, what they've read or heard about the risks, or, failing that, what they can imagine, to help them decide on the most likely order of danger.

2 When each pair has finished, allow time for them to compare their results with others and to discuss briefly any differences.

3 Finally, they should turn to the answers on page 198 and discuss the reasons for the order of risks shown there.

▶Text 1 (p. 74)

Note: Explain the use of 'dice' as a *noun* (plural) – small cubes with different numbers on each side, used in games, and as a *verb* – to gamble. Elicit the meaning of the expression 'to dice with death' in the title – to take a great risk.

Pre-questions Suggested answers

1 So that we can change public attitudes towards dangerous activities more effectively than we are doing at present.

2 The fact that people go on doing things which are dangerous to health and that, despite press campaigns, the numbers of smokers, for example, have remained the same.

3 They rely on personal experience or stories they have heard.

Multiple choice

1 A (eg title); 2 C (paragraphs 5 and 6); 3 A (lines 47–51); 4 D (lines 96–97); 5 B (lines 106–109)

Vocabulary items included in Vocabulary review

run the risk (28); contract (29); take a toll on (84)

▶Focus on grammar 1 (p. 76)

Suggested introduction

(books closed)

Write on the board: Many motorists/kill/if/not wear/seat-belts. Elicit from students the relevant sentence from Text 1 (lines 64–67) and ask them to name the type of sentence and describe its form. Check concept.

Exercise 1 – possible answers

a we would never have found our way.
b you hadn't kept your promise.
c hadn't gone swimming after lunch.
d I might have been stopped for speeding.
e they hadn't given you a pay rise?
f we wouldn't be in such a mess now.

Exercise 2

Ask students to classify each sentence 1, 2, 3a or 3b, according to the type of conditional, in addition to making the necessary changes. They will probably need to refer back to the *Focus on grammar 2* section in Unit 3 (pp. 44–45).

a hadn't fused; wouldn't have minded (3a)
b would never have kept; had had (3a)
  would never keep; had (2)
c had never met; might have married (3a)
d will not have; arrives (1)
e hadn't been watching; would certainly have heard (3a)
f wouldn't be refused; had always paid (3b)
  wouldn't have been refused; had always paid (3a)
g would you be; (hadn't) had (3b)
h would you have done; had been (3a)
i would enjoy; ate (2)
j hadn't been; might have spread (3a)

▶Text 2 (p. 77)

Ask students to explain what a hypochondriac is and how they would recognise one. Ask if they have known any hypochondriacs or if they have any hypochondriacal tendencies themselves! (an admission from the teacher might help here.) Discuss whether habitual hypochondriacs cause any problems (eg taking time off work unnecessarily/wasting doctors' time) and the best way to react to a hypochondriac's worries.

Possible pre-questions

1 How much does the writer know about medicine?
2 What kind of people are anti-hypochondriacs?
3 Underline any medical terms in the passage.

Suggested answers

1 He knows a little, perhaps more than the average man, but not enough to make reliable diagnoses.

2 They are sensible, practical people who do not suffer from hypochondria and who do not sympathise with those who do.

3 (throbbing), gangrene, doses (twitch), spasm, coronary thrombosis, duodenum, barium meal tests, pneumonia, (a swelling), cancer, lymph gland, brain tumour, paralyse, (chapped), inflammation.

Multiple choice

1 B (3–4); 2 B (throbbing/twitch/swelling – lines 5/9/18); 3 D (paragraph 4); 4 A (lines 25–26); 5 C (lines 35–38)

Vocabulary items included in Vocabulary review

throb (5); dose (8); admit of (29); mope (30); remind one of (30); for all. . . (38)

▶Focus on grammar 2 (p. 79)

Since stress and intonation are crucial, a brief drill might be appropriate.

Prompt	*Response*
I can't do that. (wish)	I ˈwish I could do that.
You weren't there. (if only)	If ˈonly you had been there.
The weather was awful. (if only)	If ˈonly the weather hadn't been so awful.
You don't keep your promises. (wish)	I ˈwish you kept your promises.
I'm not in a position to help you. (wish)	I ˈwish I were in a position to help you.
He swore at me. (If only)	If ˈonly he hadn't sworn at me.
I trod on her toes. (wish)	I ˈwish I hadn't trodden on her toes.

Exercise 1

Encourage students to give imaginative rather than routine answers.

Example answers

1 I wish/If only I had the money for a holiday in the sun!/I could escape from this office!/I had taken that job in Nassau!

2 I wish/If only you hadn't suggested this stupid picnic!/we'd listened to the weather forecast!/we'd gone to Portugal for our holidays!

3 I wish/If only I could afford a superb camera like that/he would stop showing off his new camera!

4 I wish/If only I'd stuck to my diet!/I had a figure like that!

5 I wish/If only I hadn't left the paint on the stepladder!/I hadn't jogged the stepladder!/I hadn't been too lazy to move that table out of the way!

6 I wish/If only he hadn't been such a persuasive salesman!/I hadn't let him in!/I'd pretended I was out!

This exercise can be extended with other suitable pictures (eg damaged car, burnt food/arm in a sling) and used for pairwork. One student uses 'I wish'/'If only' and the other responds appropriately: 'You should've'/'You ought to. . .'

Exercise 2

a 'd rather; wouldn't
b suppose
c it's (about/high) time
d if only
e as if
f would listen/pay attention
g I went to bed
h he were there/had been there
i didn't mention it/tell anyone else
j someone had seen you etc.

▶Text 3 (p. 81)

Pre-questions

Use the two questions to stimulate discussion on the subject, to elicit from students any personal experience they may have had, and to revise and extend topic vocabulary (eg ward, casualty department, operating theatre, outpatients department; sister, matron; dressing, bandage, sling, splint, plaster cast, etc.)

Suggested answers

1 She is expected to be completely dedicated to her job (self-sacrificing vocation), and not to suffer from normal physical, mental and emotional human failings.

2 *a* The high expectations we have of nurses in terms of their physical and mental health.
  b The nature of the work which involves dealing with death and distress among patients and relatives but requires nurses to suppress their feelings.
  c The nature of the work which involves menial tasks in difficult conditions.
  d The hierarchical system which doesn't prepare nurses for personal responsibility but still requires it of them, often without warning.

Note: Another question you could ask at this point is: 'How does the nursing profession resemble the armed forces?'

Suggested answers to questions

1 are troubled by/suffer from/are victims of

2 not to mention/to say nothing of

3 Because nurses are not expected to commit crimes.

4 Their own pain.

5 are not difficult to find.

6 Because a study proving that these actually increased anxiety was published 20 years ago.

7 it isn't acceptable for nurses to

8 That she concentrated on trivial matters, acted against the patient's real needs, and deprived the nurse of part of her job satisfaction.

9 She has been taught to obey orders rather than to take personal responsibility.

10 selected for special attention

11 They are unable to do their job properly.

12 Give marks for a well-expressed paragraph including the following points:
recognition that nurses are not super-human and suffer from the normal range of physical, mental and emotional problems.
a *breakdown* of the social defence systems which commonly operate by a) allowing nurses to express their feelings about their work, and b) encouraging more personal relationships between nurses and patients.
improving training for nurses so that they are a) better prepared for personal responsibility, and b) given more encouragement and less criticism.

Vocabulary items included in Vocabulary review

vocation (7); prey to (9); let alone (11); evasion/evasive (51); substitute for (65/66); single out (71)

▶Communication activity (p. 82)

Allow 30–40 minutes for this activity.

Preparation

Introduce the activity by explaining that it is in three parts and is designed to find out how fit a person is, and to suggest ways in which his/her fitness could be increased. Point out that all the instructions are in the book and that they should be read very carefully before each part is begun. No pair should begin a part unless they know exactly what to do and they should ask for help if necessary.

If you have made a note of the fitter and less fit students in the class (following the Lead-in), select the less fit to be interviewed! Both students can look at their books but only the interviewer should write down the information.

Pair work

Part 1

Encourage students to play the role of interviewer as creatively as possible, using a variety of question forms, rather than simply working through the list of activities in the book mechanically.

If any student does turn out to do the required amount of vigorous activity at this stage, they should swap roles with their partner straight away.

Part 2

Students may need help with some of the vocabulary – eg agile (active), trim (reduce), tone up (make stronger, more effective), ward off (prevent).

Part 3

Students may need help in following the instructions for this part. Explain that *Column 1* is to be ticked if their partner was concerned with A (Physical Fitness), B (Looks and Figure) or D (Relaxation and Social Life). *Column 2* is to be ticked if their partner was concerned with C (General Health) and *Columns 3 and 4* are both to be ticked for everyone.

Remind them to read the instructions carefully and check they are following the correct procedure.

Feedback

Finally, students can report back on the results they have had, and can discuss how convincing they are and whether they intend to follow any of the suggestions.

Vocabulary items included in Vocabulary Review

ward off

▶Focus on listening (p. 86)

Vocabulary items included in Vocabulary review

tuck in

▶Focus on writing 1 (p. 87)

Since most of the language needed for this task has already been met in the previous section, an oral preparation stage is not really necessary. However, if you feel that the students would benefit from having a model, the instructions for the first exercise could be completed orally.

Suggested answers

1 . . . and slowly bend your elbows so that your body leans towards the wall, in a straight line. Repeat four times.

2 Lie flat on your back with your knees bent and your hands clasped behind your head. Sit up fifteen times.

3 Lie flat on your back with your legs straight and your arms at your side. Raise your legs together and try to touch the floor behind your head. Hold this position for twenty seconds. Repeat.

4 Stand with your left side near a wall and place your left hand on the wall for support. Grasp your right ankle with your right hand and pull the foot up as high as possible towards your body. Lean forwards from the waist as you do this. Hold the position for twenty to thirty seconds and then repeat the exercise with the other hand and foot.

5 Sit on the floor with your right leg extended straight ahead. Bend your left knee and tuck your left foot in behind you, close to your body, so that your left thigh is at right angles to your body. Slowly slide your hands down the extended leg and try to touch your foot. Hold the position for twenty to thirty seconds and then repeat the exercise with the other leg extended.

6 Sit on the floor with your legs extended in front of you, apart. Rest your left hand on your left thigh and grasp the inside of your right foot with your right hand. Slowly lift and straighten the right leg until it is about 45 degrees from the floor. Hold the position for twenty to thirty seconds and then repeat with the other leg.

▶Focus on register (p. 88)

Vocabulary matching

a smart (1); **b** expended (1); **c** two-wheeler (1); **d** outstrips (1); **e** versatile (1); **f** under the weather (2); **g** a trifle (2); **h** sluggish (2); **i** stint (2); **j** unearthly (2); **k** hefty (2); **l** outweighed by (4); **m** briskly (4); **n** inhaling (4); **o** dispels (4); **p** trivial (4)

Multiple choice

1 C; 2 D; 3 C; 4 B; 5 A

Vocabulary items included in Vocabulary review

expend (1), outstrip (1), versatile (1), draughty (2), outweigh (4), briskly (4).

▶Focus on writing 2 (p. 90)

Remind the students of the importance of planning! A possible approach would be:

1 Choose one of the topics and elicit from the class points which could be included in an essay on that topic. Write these up on the board in random order.

2 When a good number have been suggested, ask the class to group those which belong together under sub-headings (this could be done in pairs). They should then decide on a logical ordering of paragraphs.

3 Ask students, as individuals, to see if they have any personal experience which would be relevant at any stage and also to plan a suitable introduction and conclusion to frame the essay effectively.

▶**Vocabulary practice** (p. 91)

Review

1 D (1.29)			
2 B (3.71)	**8 C** (CA)	**14 D** (3.51)	**20 A** (3.9)
3 B (1.60–61)	**9 C** (2.38)	**15 B** (3.65)	**21 C** (R1)
	10 A (L)	**16 B** (1.84)	**22 A** (R1)
4 D (1.28)	**11 B** (R2)	**17 C** (3.11)	**23 C** (R1)
5 D (R4)	**12 A** (3.7)	**18 C** (2.8)	**24 D** (2.5)
6 B (R4)	**13 A** (2.30)	**19 B** (2.19)	**25 C** (2.29)
7 C (2.30)			

Common expressions for describing ill health and injuries

Symptoms

1 dizzy; **2** swollen; **3** runny; **4** rash; **5** queasy; **6** seedy; **7** sore; **8** feverish

Injuries

1 grazed; **2** scalded; **3** blistered; **4** sprained; **5** scratch; **6** gash; **7** fractured; **8** bruises

▶**Grammar practice** (p. 94)

1 (1) cause; (2) consists; (3) which; (4) body; (5) processes; (6) much; (7) link/connection/relationship; (8) goes/dates; (9) agreement/consensus/evidence/proof; (10) failure/inability; (11) varies/differs; (12) by; (13) lead/contribute; (14) point; (15) salty; (16) its (*no* apostrophe); (17) whereas/while; (18) unknown/non-existent; (19) although/while; (20) within

2
  a *I doubt if he'll telephone* this late at night.
  b I'm sorry, *I took you for* somebody else.
  c Any correspondence from the London office *must take priority over/be given priority over* other matters. *Priority must be given to any correspondence. . .*
  d I advise you not *to place any reliance on* what you read in the papers about me.
  e Surely you *took a risk in/by hitch–hiking* all the way alone?
  f My secretary *may have taken* the order book away./*It may be that* my secretary *has taken* the order book away.
  g I'm trying to *convert these dollars into* pounds.
  h *He didn't contribute to* the conversation *at all.*
  i Let me know *the minute* you have any news.
  j This dispute is likely *to result in* a strike./The result of this dispute is likely to be a strike.

UNIT **6 Crime and Punishment**

▶**Summary of contents**

▶**Lead-in** (p. 95)

Oral introduction

1 Types of Crime
a) As individuals, students make a list of as many types of crime as possible (eg murder).
b) (Optional) Students compare lists briefly in twos or threes.
c) Teacher elicits items to put on board. These should include: theft/burglary/robbery; forgery; fraud. Check understanding.

2 Courts
a) Elicit or give the two types of court (in England and Wales) and the distinction between them:
  (i) Magistrates' – minor offences, with a maximum sentence of 12 months, tried by Justices of the Peace (JPs).
  (ii) Crown – serious cases tried before a judge and jury.
b) Introduce terms *indictable* and *non-indictable* (See Quiz question 2) and check pronunciation.

3 Punishment

a) Lead brief discussion on types of punishment available, including fines, probation and imprisonment.

b) Introduce term *criminal responsibility* and discuss, in a general way, a possible minimum age for this. (Do not reveal the age for England and Wales.)

c) (Optional) Revise the following terms with special attention to prepositions: arrested *for*, on suspicion *of*, accused *of*, charged *with*, convicted *of*, sentenced *to*.

Quiz

1 Students *either* work in pairs to complete the quiz *or* complete it individually and then compare answers.

2 Students *either* check answers on page 198 and then discuss them *or* discuss them with the teacher who supplies the correct information.

▶ Text 1 (p. 96)

Pre-Questions Suggested answers

1 Shop-lifting

2 From an armed robber, from professional shop-lifters and probably from some store detectives.

3 He learnt how shop-lifters work as a team; one preparing the goods to be stolen, one diverting attention, and the others carrying the goods away.

Multiple choice

1 D (3/4 and 11); 2 B (20–23); 3 D (Note: 'move' not 'remove' as in B); 4 A (40–42); 5 C (56–58)

Vocabulary items included in Vocabulary review

blatant (11), for my liking (11), on the (discreet) side (15/16), divert (37), in possession (42/43), dither (53)

▶ Focus on grammar 1 (p. 97)

Exercise 1

a Present participle; b Gerund; c Gerund; d Present participle (*As I was* crossing. . .); e Gerund; f Present participle (*who was* reading. . .)

Exercise 2

a can't help; b mind; c give up/stop; d denied; e recall (remember); f miss; g put off/postponed; h reported; i involve; j considered; k resist; l risk; m resent/dislike; n prevent/stop; o anticipated

Exercise 3

a turning (switching) off/having turned (switched) off
b of taking
c trying/attempting
d not calling/'phoning
e with demanding
f to taking
g of his giving up/abandoning
h on being chosen/selected
i at missing/having missed/not having had
j from applying
k making
l of interfering
m to hearing
n in making
o from changing

▶ Text 2 (p. 100)

Pre-questions Suggested answers

1 They are a group of volunteers in New York who help protect the public from crime.

2 They patrol public places such as streets, parks and subways to discourage criminals or to arrest them after a crime has been committed.

3 Because the crime rate in New York has been increasingly rapid in recent years.

Vocabulary matching

a borne the brunt of (1/2); b notorious (11); c swarthy (15); d wields (20); e incarnate (24); f gall (24); g thwarted (30); h assaults (30); i maintains (31) (claims (28)); j makeup (35)

Multiple choice

1 B (49/50); 2 B (24/26); 3 C (40–42); 4 A (44); 5 C (61/62)

Vocabulary items included in Vocabulary review

wields (20), make an arrest (31) deterrent (50), coverage (54), adherence/adhere (69)

▶ Focus on grammar 2 (p. 102)

Exercise 1

to spend; combating; to be trained/being trained; going; to live; providing; to build; introducing; learn; to face; meeting; to receive; being allowed; to be accompanied/being accompanied; supervised; adopting; keeping

Exercise 2

1 leave

2 to be so congested

3 know/see how nervous she was

4 working from 6pm till midnight

5 imply that it was all my fault

6 really need to be typed

7 your voting for me

8 with (all) your complaining/your continual complaining

▶ Focus on writing 1 (p. 103)

An oral introduction to one or both options would be useful. Suggestions can be elicited and passive vocabulary activated – eg (Option 2) *cell, wing, block, exercise yard, bars, bolt/unbolt; prison warder, prison governor, sentence, remission, solitary confinement,* etc.

▶ Communication activity (p. 104)

Allow 40–50 minutes for this activity.

Note: It is useful, but not essential, to have two rooms available for this activity.

Preparation

1 Check understanding of situation and procedure.

2 Select suspects (two for each group) and police inspectors (2–4 for each group). Weaker students should work with stronger ones as police inspectors.

3 Each pair of suspects reads their instructions and works out an alibi *while* each group of police inspectors reads their instructions and discusses suitable questions.

4 Check with suspects that they have noted all the information in their instructions. Encourage them to think of imaginative activites and to work out all the details they might be questioned on (eg name of film, cinema; price of ticket; length of film; interval? etc.).

5 Check with police inspectors that they, too, have read and remembered all the details in their instructions. Suggest a possible alibi, eg a meal in a restaurant, and go through a number of the possible questions they could ask: eg How much was the bill? Could you tell us who paid it? Would you mind telling us whether you paid in cash or by cheque? Do you remember exactly where you sat? Did you have wine with the meal?

Role play

1 Arrange groups so that police inspectors face suspects, either across a table or in a small circle. Groups should be well separated. While the first suspect is being interviewed, the second must be out of earshot (outside if necessary). Remind police inspectors of the 10 minute time limit.

2 After about 10 minutes, swap suspects. Again the unoccupied suspect should be out of earshot and could observe another interview.

3 Check on the progress of the interviews but there should be be no need to intervene unless police inspectors run out of questions, in which case whispered or written suggestions could be given.

Note errors of structure, lexis or pronunciation.

4 At the end of the second 10 minutes, the two suspects in each group can discuss their interviews while the police inspectors decide on a verdict.

5 Police inspectors give their verdict and reasons to suspects.

Feedback

1 Students can read the instructions for the role they didn't play and give their reactions to the activity.
2 Remedial work can be done on question forms and other areas of weakness noted during the role play.

▶ Language Check (p. 104)

Dependent Prepositions 4: Verb + Preposition

benefit **from**
charge somebody **with** something
cheat somebody **out of** something
compliment somebody **on**
concentrate **on**
confess **to**
convince somebody **of** something
deprive somebody **of**

differ **from**
disapprove **of**
plead guilty **to**
prevent somebody/something **from**
rob somebody **of**
specialise **in**
suspect somebody **of**
threaten somebody **with**

▶ Focus on listening (p. 105)

DEVICE	NUMBER	POWER: M – Mains B – Battery	VOLUME in decibels	PRICE
ultra-sonic burglar alarm	7	M B	85	£80
do-it-yourself burglar alarm	6	B	✗	£138
infra-red burglar alarm	1	B	97	£130
portable door alarm	3	B	95	£6·50
personal attack/door alarm	2	B	110	£8·00
personal attack alarm	4	B	✗	£3·99

Lexis

device; break-in; boom business; emit, screech; strike a deal; dismantle[R]; trigger; siren; install[R]/installation; set off; plug into; mains; unobtrusive; squeeze

[R]included in Vocabulary review.

▶ Focus on register (p. 106)

When checking the matching exercise, ask students to say which words from the headlines and extracts led them to the answers.

Extract 1–Headline E (burglar/break into, steal)
Extract 2–Headline C (Chips–but could there be two meanings?)
Extract 3–Headline D (Luggage tags, burglars/Heathrow, travellers, crooks)
Extract 4–Headline B (Gem, auction/diamond, sale)
Extract 5–Headline A (A-Level)

Ask students to speculate about the meaning of the other unknown words, eg *bungling, switch, downfall, conman, Yard,* but don't confirm or deny any suggestions.

Multiple choice

1 Extract 2; 2 Extracts 3 and 5; 3 Extract 5; 4 Extract 2; 5 Extract 4

Vocabulary items included in Vocabulary review

bungling/bungle (E) haul (1), flaw (2), proceeds (2), monitoring (4), sit (an examination) (5), seething (5), lax (5).

▶ Focus on grammar 3 (p. 109)

Refer students to the Focus on grammar sections 1 and 2 on pages 97 and 102 in this Unit.

Exercise

A to make; feeling
B to be; to do; joining; having; going; attending; to say
A attending; to persevere; spending; sharing; to think
B doing/to be done; to think
A giving; meeting; to make; to invite; going; seeing
B to come; to ring

▶ Focus on writing 2 (p. 110)

This is suitable for homework or timed essay practice in class without any oral introduction. Remind students of the importance of making notes and planning the structure beforehand, and, if necessary, refer them back to the suggestions made in previous Focus on writing sections. You could have a preparation session and check notes before students begin the essay.

►Vocabulary practice (p. 110)

Review

1 C (2.28)	**8** B (L)	**14** A (2.42)	**20** B (FoG 1 Ex
2 A (L)	**9** B (1.15/	**15** C (1.37)	3)
3 C (RE)	16)	**16** B (R1)	**21** C (R2)
4 B (2.19)	**10** A (1.42/	**17** B (1.11)	**22** D (R5)
5 D (2.45)	43)	**18** D (R2 &	**23** B (R5)
6 C	**11** B (2.60)	4)	**24** D (FoG)
7 C (1.53)	**12** C (1.11)	**19** D (R4)	**25** A (R5)
	13 C (L)		

Phrasal verbs: GET

1 got round to; **2** gets by; **3** get out of; **4** get on; **5** got over; **6** get through; **7** gets me down; **8** get round; **9** getting at; **10** get away with

Grammar practice (p. 113)

1 (1) due; (2) pointed/points; (3) report; (4) reputation/character; (5) little/small; (6) afforded; (7) time/point; (8) guilty/accused; (9) raises/poses; (10) whether; (11) off; (12) concerned; (13) paid; (14) immaterial/irrelevant/unimportant; (15) once/if/when; (16) position/situation; (17) able; (18) suggest/advise/obtain; (19) offender; (20) lacking/without

2 *a* better call at the/withdraw some from the
b if/though you've seen a
c can/will we send
d my/me calling/dropping in
e minor/trivial an
f took me
g have lost
h hadn't tried to move/lift
i it sounds/may seem/seems
j to taking

UNIT **7 Learning and teaching**

►Summary of contents

►Lead-in (p. 114)

Optional preliminary activity

Ask students to write down what they *most* enjoyed (enjoy) about school and what they *least* enjoyed (enjoy). Discuss results briefly before starting Unit 7.

Photographs

Use these to:

a stimulate memories and get students talking about their personal experiences.

b stimulate discussion about more general issues, eg pupil/teacher relationships; class sizes; discipline; school uniforms, etc.

c practise description for the first part of the interview. This should include clothes, facial expression, mood/atmosphere, and details of furniture or background.

d revise and extend topic vocabulary.

What makes a good teacher?

Discuss the four ideas briefly, and consider possible qualifications, eg a good teacher knows his/her subject very well and can also *communicate* this knowledge to others. A good teacher always prepares his/her lessons but doesn't stick to them too *rigidly* and can *respond flexibly* to the needs of the class.

Discuss the suggestions resulting from pairwork. Find out if any students have experience of teaching of any kind.

▶Text 1 (p. 115)

Pre-questions Suggested answers

1 They are teenage pupils who have difficulties at school.

2 They are primary school children.

3 To help the primary school children to learn to read and to give the teenagers the practice they need in reading, in a motivating and satisfying way.

4 Very successful. The younger children learn to read more effectively than with any other new teaching method and the older pupils concentrate more and read more expressively than they did in class. The teenagers also develop a sense of responsibility and worth.

Multiple choice

1 C (26/27); 2 A (43); 3 B (45–48); 4 D; 5 C (34, 96–100)

Vocabulary items included in Vocabulary review

emerge (2); innovation (10/11); fall behind (26); lose face (43); struggling (45); conscientious (78); dismissed (84).

▶Focus on grammar 1 (p. 117)

a defining; b non-defining; c defining; d non-defining; e defining; f non-defining; g non-defining h defining; i non-defining.

Exercise 1

a A non-defining (There was only one dry cleaner's and it had a 2 hour service.)
  B defining (Several dry cleaners but only one with a 2 hour service.)

b A defining (Only those commuters who had heard about the derailment made other arrangements.)
  B non-defining (All the commuters had heard about the derailment and so made other arrangements.)

c A non-defining (All the cars had been double-parked and so were towed away.)
  B defining (Only those cars which had been double-parked were towed away.)

Exercise 2

a The book you borrowed. . ./The book that you borrowed. . .

b We called at a pub that is said to be. . .

c No change

d the travel agency you deal with. . ./the travel agency that you deal with. . .

e No change

Exercise 3

a Toledo, which is a very fine city to visit, gets extremely hot in summer.

b The tent (which/that) you lent me was damaged in the storm (which/that) you heard about on the news.

c The woman who lives next door bought an Old English Sheepdog which barks all night.

d The price of petrol, which rose only last month, is going up again.

e We rented a cottage from a man who has written a novel which/that has become a best seller.

f The letters (which/that) I asked you to type for me are full of careless errors.

g The zoo's most famous panda, whose name was Chi Chi, has died.

h The record (that) I told you about, which has been produced by a completely new method, will be released next week.

▶Text 2 (p. 119)

Suggested lead-in

Ask students *either* to tell you their reasons for being in the class *or* to ask their neighbour and report back. Categorise the various reasons on the board according to whether they are mainly academic, professional, social, or result from some other factor such as parental duress!

Pre-questions Suggested answers

1 Firstly, to enable us to read, write and handle figures; secondly, to enable us to get a job and earn a living.

2 The second reason might no longer apply. A new motive for learning will have to be found.

3 Because of the competitive society in which we live, which makes us used to striving against other people, rather than against ourselves.

4 The fact that evening classes are well-attended and that her own experience has been successful.

Vocabulary matching

a resolves itself (3–4); b soul-searching (7); c cope (8); d obsolete (20); e reshuffle (52); f the furniture of our minds (52–3); g gear. . . .towards (53–4); h keeping up with the Joneses (55); i spurs (57); j integrate (61); k pitting. . . against (74)

Multiple choice

1 C (24–28); 2 C (40, 60–62); 3 A (51–57); 4 D (88–90); 5 A (104–107)

Vocabulary items included in Vocabulary review

resolved (3), obsolete (20), with a view to (25), nevertheless (50), redress (85), glimpse (98), elusive (101), stumbling (108).

▶Focus on writing 1 (p. 120)

This can seem a daunting task initially, and an oral introduction is useful in helping students to (a) 'read' the four tables, (b) identify the most significant results, and (c) consider the implications. This can be done by simple question and answer.

eg for *The aims for education:*

1 Which aim was chosen by most parents and children? (The second)

2 How many parents? (About half); How many children? (About three out of four)

3 What were the results for the teachers? (They were almost equally divided between the other two aims.)

4 Which group produced the most decisive result? (The children)

5 Can you think why so few teachers should have chosen the second aim, compared with parents and children? (Perhaps they have a more realistic view of the employment situation.)

6 Which group was least sure of the aims of education? (The teachers); How do you react to this result?

Reinforce the points made in the student's book regarding the need for *organisation* and *interpretation* rather than mechanical reproduction of every detail. Marking should obviously reflect this.

▶Text 3 (p. 122)

Suggested lead-in

1 Ask students what provisions there are in their country/ies for adults who want to study in their spare time. Can they attend leisure classes such as Photography or Cookery as well as more academic ones? Are classes available to everyone? How much do they cost? Where are they generally held?

2 Describe the situation in Britain briefly. This is explained and exemplified in the Communication Activity in this unit.

Optional pre-question

What do we learn about the students who attend the history class?

Suggested answer

Many of them are tired after a day's work and need frequent breaks; some have specialised knowledge of the subject and may make things difficult for the tutor; some are so enthusiastic that they take a lot of the tutor's time but it is they who really keep the class going.

Vocabulary matching

a set upon (8); b far from (10); c miscreant (11); d keen (20); e awkward (25); f (known) authority (26–27); g roused (28); h ruminations (28); i putting paid to (32); j dwindling (33)

Suggested answers to questions

1 He imagines that the late-comer is physically attacked, karate-style, by his fellow students.

2 Because the information it contains sounds so boring.

3 Offering the promise of rewards.

4 He is more knowledgeable than the tutor in certain specialised aspects of the subject and could contradict some of the tutor's statements, which would be embarrassing.

5 destroying

6 They listen extremely attentively to what the tutor has to say.

7 That the tutor is not really interested in the fossils and rather dreads the day when they are brought in.

8 They react with excited anticipation despite the unpromising material./They act as though the dreary old documents offered the most exciting prospect imaginable.

9 A small section of students are extremely keen and, perhaps, a little eccentric.

10 So that the more difficult students will have left.

11 He suggests that they find the trip a welcome change from the more serious environment of the classroom.

12 Because they don't follow the recommended route but spread out over private land. They have stopped at several pubs on the way and have probably had quite a bit to drink.

13 Give marks for a well-expressed and appropriate paragraph including the following points:
   a Students can be unpunctual, tired after day's work. Need to give them coffee breaks and rest periods.
   b Some students especially knowledgeable. Could be difficult unless carefully handled.
   c Others so keen that they can be tiresome. Remember they keep class going. They are fascinated by original documents!
   d The field trip is generally popular. Danger of stopping at pubs on the way! Need to control students' tendency to reckless exploration.

Vocabulary items included in Vocabulary review

keen(ly) (20), at the drop of a *hat* (30/31), dwindle (33), *hang on. . .* every word (42), *yet* another (43), prod (56), rash(ly) (68), take *kindly* to (69/70), element (76), doomed (78).

▶Language check (p. 123)

Dependent Prepositions 5: Adjective + Preposition

according **to**	expert **at/in**
aimed **at**	far **from**
aware **of**	ignorant **of**
capable **of**	interested **in**
confined **to**	peculiar **to**
content **with** something	preferable **to**
critical **of**	proud **of**
envious **of**	sympathetic **towards**

▶Focus on grammar 2 (p. 124)

Exercise 1

a Seeing that she was on the verge of tears. . . (Reason)
b He arrived rather late, having been held up. . . (Reason)
c The weather being unsettled, we decided. . . (Reason)
d Having heard about the hi-jack on the news, I phoned . . . (Reason)
e The luggage having been unloaded, we all disappeared. . . (Time)
f Not having been given the right flight number, I had difficulty in finding out. . . (Reason)
g Approaching the final bend, the car skidded. . . (Time)
h Contracts having been exchanged, you will be free to move. . . (Time)
i Being unwilling to offer any more for the painting. . . (Reason)
j Having recieved his last minute instructions, he set off. (Time)

Exercise 2

a It appears that *we* were wearing a striped T-shirt! We thought that, wearing a striped T-shirt, he was rather casually dressed for an interview.

b It appears that *I* have been designed as a racing bike! As the bicycle had been designed for racing, I found it very smooth and easy to handle.

c It appears that *the car* wasn't looking where it was going! As he wasn't looking where he was going, the car almost hit him as he was crossing the road.

d It appears that *the letter* had learnt German! As I had learnt German at school, the letter presented no particular problem for me to translate.

e It appears that *the paella* was not hungry! As I wasn't starving hungry, the huge helping of paella was more than I could manage.

▶ Communication activity (p. 125)

Allow about 45 minutes for this activity.

Note: If this activity is done before Text 3, use the suggested lead-in for that. If not, simply remind students of the main points.

Preparation

1 Decide on the pairs who will work together and allot roles. Role B is probably best suited to the most confident speakers.

2 Students read through their role play notes for a few minutes and then form two groups to discuss their tasks in detail.

3 Those with Role A should speculate about the courses and discuss the kinds of questions they should ask in order to elicit the information they need.

4 When you visit the groups, check that they are clear about the points to bear in mind. (eg When are they free to come to classes? What is the earliest time they could attend? etc.) Make sure, too, that they are prepared to ask a variety of questions in a natural way, using the handwritten notes for guidance only. Tell them they will have to choose one class and remind them to keep an open mind!

5 Those with Role B should decide what notes, if any, they need to make on the list (eg reminders about classes marked*; symbols for classes where fees could be paid by instalments, etc.) They should also discuss any problems of comprehension.

When you visit the group, check that they are quite clear about the instructions and remind them of the need for persuasion and dissuasion!

Role play

1 The most suitable arrangement for this activity is for students to sit facing each other, one on each side of a desk or table.

2 Student B should begin as if he/she has just walked in and sat down. (eg 'Hello. I'm interested in joining an evening class and I wonder if you could give me some more information about the ones you're offering. . .')

3 Once the role play has started, monitor unobtrusively and be prepared to help any pairs who come across a problem. Check that those with Role B are interpreting the material creatively – that they are not simply reading out the information but are using their imagination where appropriate and attempting to persuade effectively. Check that those with Role A are keeping the details of their role in mind and asking plenty of questions.

Feedback

1 Check on the decisions which have been taken and ask pairs to report back briefly on their conversations. How helpful did the Adult Education supervisors seem? How open-minded were the prospective students?

2 Ask what language they felt they lacked and include a brief practice phase of relevant language items.

▶ Focus on writing 2 (p. 126)

Though it appears simple, this is quite a demanding task in terms of clarity and precision of expression. It might be helpful to go through an example beforehand, eg cleaning a pair of shoes. Elicit suggestions for instructions and point out any crucial omissions (eg quantity of polish, need to rub in evenly all over, etc.), which could lead to unsatisfactory results. Alternatively, ask the class to give you instructions for an action (eg riding a bicycle) from the list and then play the 'innocent', taking each instruction absolutely literally and showing where mistakes could occur, (eg facing the wrong way, not knowing how to stop, etc.).

▶ Focus on listening (p. 126)

1 D; 2 C; 3 A; 4 B; 5 B

6 *Expenses*

Item	Cost
Fees	£133
Summer School	£87
Books	£5–£6

7 *Hours of study per week*

	Recommended	Actual
	15	10

8 *Times of Open University Television Programmes*

	Thursday	Sunday
	7.20–7.45 a.m.	8.55–9.20 a.m.

Lexis

mature student; compulsive; giggle; aspiring; draw a blank with; put across; send someone up (slang); fluff (an exam); make a hash of; frame of mind; apathetic; jump at a chance

▶ Focus on register (p. 128)

1 B; 2 A; 3 C; 4 C; 5 B

▶ Focus on writing 3 (p. 129)

1 Remind students of the need to make notes and plan the structure of the essay.

2 Suggest that they refer back to the tables shown in Focus on writing 1 (pp. 120 and 121) to see if there is any information which could be usefully included.

►Vocabulary practice (p. 130)

Review

1 C (1.43)	**8** C (3.42)	**14** C (1.84)	**20** D (2.20)
2 B (1.2)	**9** A (3.33)	**15** D (1.26)	**21** B (3.68)
3 D (2.3)	**10** B (3.69/70)	**16** A (1.78)	**22** B (3.30/31)
4 C (2.25)	**11** C (3.76)	**17** B (2.98)	**23** D (3.43)
5 B (1.45)	**12** A (3.56)	**18** D (2.101)	**24** A (3.78)
6 D (2.50)	**13** B (1.10/11)	**19** A (2.85)	**25** D (3.20)
7 A (2.108)			

Colloquial expressions using animal names as verbs

1 hared; **2** monkeying; **3** wolfed; **4** hogging; **5** beavering; **6** wormed; **7** dogged; **8** beetling; **9** swan; **10** foxes

►Grammar practice (p. 132)

1 (1) less; (2) has; (3) events; (4) after; (5) way; (6) seem/appear; (7) pick; (8) did; (9) shown/suggested/indicated/found; (10) improving/increasing; (11) Since; (12) by; (13) every; (14) even; (15) occurred; (16) reasons/explanations; (17) greater/wider; (18) ignored/overlooked; (19) influence/affect; (20) to

2 *a you wore* something more formal to work.
  b have I drunk worse coffee (than this)/such a bad cup of coffee.
  c being friendly with him, I hardly even know him.
  d been for your sound advice, . . .
  e must not/is not to be touched. . .
  f I was getting home.
  g the tennis match someone stole my handbag.
  h a 90-minute journey. . .
  i give me plenty of warning. . .
  j older he grows/got, *the more forgetful* he became.

UNIT **8 The Media**

►Summary of contents

►Lead-in (p. 133)

Pictures

Even such simple drawings as these can provide useful practice in describing people and their surroundings, and in speculating about the background to a scene.

Ask students to study each picture and then: (a) describe the scene in *as much detail as possible*, and (b) speculate about the people shown and the circumstances eg **Picture B**: There are two people, a man and a woman, sitting side by side in armchairs and watching a television programme very intently. The man is slightly balding and is wearing glasses. His elbows are resting on the arms of his chair and his hands are clasped loosely in front of his face. The woman looks a bit younger and has medium length blonde hair. She has her left elbow on the arm of the chair and seems to be resting her chin on her hand.

They *are probably* husband and wife and I *would imagine* that they are in their living room at home because it *seems* very domestic with the bowl of flowers on the television set and the covers on the backs of their chairs. On the other hand, I *suppose they could* be in a hotel lounge. There's an announcer on the television screen and he *might well be* reading the evening news because we can see a clock face which shows 9 o'clock in the top left hand corner of the screen. They *look* particularly interested *as if* they were waiting to hear about an event which affected them personally. *Perhaps* they've got a son in the army in some trouble spot and they're expecting a report from that area. . . etc.

Questions

Ask students to answer the first two questions individually and then discuss their results and reasons.

Discuss questions 3 and 4 as a class: 3 – immediacy, in-depth coverage, visual impact, background information, etc; 4 – order of priority, time/space allowed, selection of facts/pictures/quotations, commentary, etc.

(*Note:* this activity can be reserved as a lead-in to Text 2.)

Pair work

Discuss briefly the positive and negative effects which pairs have listed. Ask if anyone has direct experience of any of these effects or has read any reports on the subject.

▶Text 1 (p. 134)

Suggested lead-in

Ask if anyone knows anything about Randolph Hearst or *Citizen Kane*. Explain briefly that Randolph Hearst was an American newspaper proprietor (1863–1951) who became famous as the owner of the world's largest chain of newspapers. (Just after the First World War he owned 31 newspapers and 6 magazines, among many other interests!) He had his own castle built at San Simeon in California and the film *Citizen Kane*, starring Orson Welles, was based on his life story.

Optional pre-questions

1 What seems to have been the style of his newspapers?
2 What personal use did he put his newspapers to?
3 What do we learn about his personality?
4 Why was Victor Matthews, another newspaper proprietor, so pleased with his reception from the Press?

Suggested answers

1 They seem to have been rather sensational.

2 He used them to support his efforts to enter political life.

3 That he was shy, unsure of himself in public and lonely.

4 Because he was made to feel important.

Multiple choice

1 C (5–6); 2 D (15–17 etc); 3 C (25–26); 4 A (33); 5 B (45–47)

Vocabulary items included in Vocabulary review

startle (2), disregard for (5), vehicle for (7), within a(n). . . of (10), circulation (13), futile (17), lure (22), glamour (22), veteran (25), go down well (33), afford (42).

▶Text 2 (p. 136)

Suggested lead-in

Either use the pairwork activity from the lead-in to this unit, if it has been reserved, *or* initiate a discussion on the topic: favourite and least favourite types of programmes; value in terms of education/information/entertainment/escapism; harmful effects, etc.

Refer students to the questions on p. 137 *before* they start reading.

General questions

1 No, because there is no scientific evidence that this is the case.

2 Slightly less keen; the introduction of colour television.

3 Not very successful. We remember very little of what we watch.

4 For entertainment, relaxation and escapism.

5 It reduces the impact of each item they watch.

6 Because they recognise that it is different from real life.

7 Convenience (versatility).

Vocabulary matching

a monstrous (2)
b vicious (10)
c sloppy (11)
d not a scrap of (12)
e the box (16)
f advent (19)
g is breaking (23)
h detractors (25)
i diligent (27)
j impressionable (33)
k brutality (62)
l intact (62)

Suggested answers to questions

1 They pretend to be concerned about the effects of television on children while they themselves have developed a serious dependence on it.

2 Because they were expecting to hear concrete evidence of the bad effects of television but none has been produced.

3 They were wildly enthusiastic about it/It was like an unreasoning passion.

4 They have a dependence on television (as on a drug) but are able to control their addiction.

5 To know that bad programmes are not too harmful.

6 It is a completely passive activity which requires no conscious effort and produces no results. It's a way of killing time.

7 are unaffected/unchanged

8 The effects of television are also counteracted by

9 That he is undiscriminating. He doesn't care what he watches.

10 make callous or unfeeling

11 That television screens are continually talking at the viewer, regardless of whether there is anything important to say.

12 That books are a more versatile medium and more convenient to use.

13 Give marks for a well-expressed paragraph including the following points: No evidence of either good or bad results; television hasn't succeeded in educating viewers (adults or children); it encourages a passive response/basically a way of killing time; the quantity of viewing reduces the impact; both children and adults recognise that television is different from life; no convincing scientific evidence of harmful effects on children.

Vocabulary items included in Vocabulary review

take one's mind off (4), a scrap (12), infatuation (18), the former (31), intact (62), gifted (68).

►Focus grammar 1 (p. 139)

Before starting the section, ask students how the future is expressed in English. The chances are that they'll suggest the Future Simple. If this is the case, ask them to talk about one or two plans for the weekend (eg I'll write a letter) and ask how natural the form sounds. What forms would be more likely to be used? When *do* we use the Future Simple?

Ask students to cover the right hand page, as instructed, and to describe the attitude towards the future which each example illustrates. Check answers for each section as you go along and ask students to suggest more examples of their own.

Exercise

(Check *attitude/concept* in each case)

a I'm going to sell (intention)
b he'll have (prediction)
c you'll have heard (strong probability)
d Will you be taking (as a matter of course)
   Are you going to take (intention)
e I will do (promise)
f we will have been waiting (action will have occurred)
g Will you take (request)
   we will be able to (future fact)
h she's going to faint (probability based on present evidence)
i I'll call (threat)
j that'll be (strong probability)
k will be publishing (as a matter of course)
l he'll become (assumption/prediction)
m he'll have been giving (strong probability)
n will we have to (future fact)
o will have been moving (action will have occurred)
p are you going to do (intention)
   will admit (opinion)
q you will be able to (opinion)
r won't be having. . . will (action in progress)
s won't go (refusal)
   I'll deal (sudden decision)
t will you have had (action will have occurred)

►Communication activity (p. 141)

(Allow about an hour for this activity.)
Note: Don't be put off by the slightly complicated-sounding instructions! This activity works well and is relatively straightforward to organise as long as the teacher is clear about procedure. It's obviously important to have read the instructions and notes below beforehand so that operations flow smoothly.

There are four basic stages *1 Preparation, 2 Practice Interviews, 3 Real Interviews, 4 Feedback.* If there are no tape recorders available, and time is limited, stage 2 can be omitted. This does, however, reduce the role of the assistants a little.

Preparation

1 Decide which students should work together (a team consists of 1 guest, 1 interviewer and 1 or 2 assistants), and allot roles. The role of assistant is probably best suited to the weaker students.

2 Give students time to read through the notes for their roles and then ask all the interviewers to form a group. Allow guests time to choose a topic and formulate their ideas while you explain to the assistants how the tape recorder(s) operate(s). If tape recorders are not used, assistants can have a brief discussion about the questions they are going to ask. Start preliminary interviews between assistants and guests.

3 Interviewers discuss suitable introductions and conclusions to the programme, the questions they should ask, and the time limit.
   When you visit the group, check that the time limit is realistic (about 10 minutes) and suggest some topics for them to design leading questions for.

4 Assistants (individually or in pairs) interview guests and note down basic information. Monitor progress and, in particular, the appropriate formulation of questions.

Practice interviews

(This stage can be omitted. See introductory note.)

1 Each team should form a small group and groups should be as well-separated from each other as possible.

2 Remind assistants that they have an important role here and that they should note down any suggestions they have for improvements, especially in the questioning technique.

3 Monitor proceedings but only comment or advise if absolutely necessary.

Real interviews

1 If practice interviews have been held, arrange for assistants to swap groups.

2 If tape recorders are used, make sure that these are in a suitable place and that the assistant remembers to make a brief test recording. Stay apart from proceedings.

3 If tape recorders are not used, the teacher should observe part of each interview but *not* interfere in any way.

Feedback

1 Play recordings back/and or ask assistants to report on the success of the interviews they've observed. They could comment on how interesting the final interview was, how successful the interviewer was at putting his/her guest at ease, and how effective the questions were in keeping the conversation going.

2 Do some remedial language work, if appropriate.

►Focus on listening (p. 143)

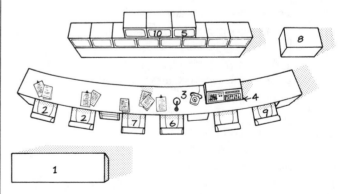

Multiple choice

2 A (lighting. . . subdued); 3 B; 4 B (a key person); 5 B

Lexis

nerve centre; a bird's eye view; the set; subdued; glare; a bank of; cubicle; a barrage of

▶Focus on grammar 2 (p. 144)

Exercise

Ask students to underline time links in each sentence.

a He'll see *before* he gets
b You are to report *until* your case comes up
c I'll drive/I'm driving/I'm going to drive *as* he steps off
d I'll give *just as soon as* I've had
e they are not to go *till* they have tidied
f We'll have done *once* we get
g The train arrives *(as* is not a time link here) my boyfriend is meeting I won't need
h Are you doing
my mother is coming *after* she leaves I'll try/I'm going to try

▶Focus on writing (p. 144)

This topic may seem daunting at first and some form of preliminary discussion is advisable. For example:

1 In pairs or small groups, students list as many different types of programmes as possible, under the three headings.

2 General discussion of the three questions (under Notes) in relation to the results of the pair/group work.

3 Remind students of the need for a clear, logical structure (based on notes) and for an appropriate introduction and conclusion.

▶Language Check (p. 145)

Just

1 g; **2** d; **3** j; **4** b; **5** e; **6** a; **7** i; **8** f; **9** c; **10** h

▶Focus on register (p. 145)

Headline pairing exercise

Instruct students to cover page 147 while doing this task.

1. 'Lazy' doc gets a rap (f)
Fined for refusing car patient (c)

BEV HITS ROOF AT NO-GIRLS JOB BAN (g)
Woman wins sex bias case (h)

ALL-OUT STRIKE (d)
Day the jailbirds came out in sympathy (e)

'Shoplift slur' on Doris, 72 (a)
Shop sued over Christmas card arrest (j)

Crackdown on crooks (b)
Home Sec. to back tough sentences (i)

Headline/article matching exercise

1A (e); **2A** (h); **3A** (i); **4A** (c); **5A** (j); **1B** (d); **2B** (g); **3B** (b); **4B** (f)

Multiple choice

1 C (came out in sympathy)

2 D (hits the roof)

3 B (crackdown)

4 A (a rap)

5 C (slur)

6 A (austerity measures)

7 C (It stems from. . . advice from women)

8 C (hardline)

9 B (the doctor could not make an examination. . . noise from the traffic/no reasonable excuse)

10 D (browsed through back issues)

Comparing the different treatments

Possible answers

1 The police appeal about clothes on clothes line and the reason for it; the method of escape, the scale of the search, the reason for the warders' strike, etc.

2 That readers of popular newspapers are not expected to be interested in foreign news beyond the bare facts.

3 Headline (b) uses two slang expressions and gives little indication as to the content of the article – 'crackdown' could refer to increased efforts to catch criminals, as well as to severe sentences, for example. Headline (i) is far more informative and uses two jargon words, but no slang.

4 The fact that a passer-by had made several attempts to persuade the doctor to examine the man. It strengthens the case considerably.

Vocabulary items included in Vocabulary review

appealed, elapsed (1A); crumbled, stem from (2A); alert (4A); damages, browse through (5A); all-out (d)

▶Vocabulary practice (p. 150)

1 D (2.3/4)	**8** C (1.22)	**14** D (1.22)	**20** B (R 5A)
2 B (2.12)	**9** B (1.42)	**15** A (1.7)	**21** A (R 4A)
3 D (2.31)	**10** B (1.33)	**16** C (1.17)	**22** A (R 5A)
4 A (2.68)	**11** C (1.13)	**17** A (1.7)	**23** B (R 2A)
5 B (2.62)	**12** A (1.10)	**18** C (R 1A)	**24** D (R 1A)
6 C (2.18)	**13** C (1.15)	**19** D (R 2A)	**25** B (R d)
7 D (1.2)			

Phrasal verbs: PUT

1 put you off	**5** put you out	**8** put me up
2 put forward	**6** put the	**9** put it about
3 put it down	meeting off	**10** putting it
4 put up with	**7** put across	on

▶Grammar practice (p. 152)

1 (1) intervals; (2) as; (3) go; (4) able; (5) cannot; (6) over; (7) Other/Further; (8) content; (9) differ; (10) giving; (11) differences; (12) printed/produced; (13) together; (14) drawn; (15) form/format; (16) exist; (17) cater; (18) concerned; (19) in; (20) include

2 *a* He has *the reputation of (being)/a reputation as*. . .
b I made an offer for the premises next door *with a view to* expand*ing* my shop.
c *Children and adults alike* will enjoy this game.
d The prisoner was recaptured as he *made a dash for* the gate.
e This particular wine *is considered (to be)* one of the finest in the world.
f Since the company's methods were exposed in a newspaper, it *has fallen into disrepute*.
g What really *gets me down* is. . .
h We missed the bus *as a consequence of* over-sleep*ing*.
i She *let it be known* that she was looking for a flat.
j They *persisted in suggesting* that. . .

UNIT 9 Science and Technology

►Summary of contents

►Lead-in (p. 154)

First part

No introduction is needed. General discussion is best to follow pair work.

1 Encourage students to think *not only* about the importance of each invention in modern day life *but also* about the significance each had at the time when it first appeared, and about later developments which each led to.

Collate results and discuss reasons in detail.

2 A good opportunity for practising Type 3 Conditionals (with both past and present results – see Unit 5 Focus on grammar 1). This practice can be focused to a greater or lesser extent, depending on the needs of the students.

Second part

1 Before beginning the pairwork, and with students' books closed, focus on the language needed for the two tasks:

a) *Static description of objects*
   eg it's shaped like a. . . /it's. . . in shape
      circular/rectangular; horizontal/vertical
   it consists of/it's made of
   supported by; suspended from;
   attached to/fixed to/connected to. . . by etc.
   These language items could be practised using classroom objects or furniture, or suitable pictures of objects.

b) *speculation*
   eg it may/might/could be
      it seems to be/have
      it looks like a. . .
      it looks as if it. . .

Suitably ambiguous pictures or drawings would be useful practice material.

2 Discuss results of pairwork, encouraging reported speculation (eg 'We thought it might be. . .') and revising descriptive terms, before moving on to the matching exercise.

Matching exercise

This is best done individually but students should check their results with others as soon as they've finished.

Picture	Headline	Text
1	B	5
2	D	2
3	E	1
4	C	3
5	A	4

Check answers and, in particular, the part of the text which matched the headline and drawing.

Questions

1 Two circular apertures (? = holes) in the lid.

2 It's covered by a dressing table top so that it looks like a piece of furniture.

3 The lifting power created by the four propellers.

4 The discomfort caused by the shaking of the train.

5 Because the 'rider's' feet are off the ground. It's like walking on stilts.

6 Because unless the brake on the front wheel is applied, it would continue to move forwards and the rider's legs would shoot apart, causing him to land on the ground most uncomfortably!

►Text 1 (p. 157)

1 A (8/9); **2 C** (4/5, 12); **3 B** (15–16)

In reviewing this text, check why the airship, radio etc might have been invented too early – ie what advantages they might have over later developments and why we might overlook them.

Vocabulary items included in Vocabulary review

come adrift (15)

▶Text 2 (p. 158)

Optional lead-in

Ask students to say what robots are, what uses they have, when they were first introduced and why their introduction is sometimes resisted. Check the meaning of the idiom 'a spanner in the works'.

Pre-questions

1 Origin

2 Ability

3 Uses/Applications

4 Limitations

5 Arguments against potential developments in robots

6 Arguments for potential developments in robots

7 Summing up of two arguments

Vocabulary matching

a came into being (3/4); **b** mundane (4); **c** booming (5); **d** advent (18); **e** uncanny (22); **f** layman (23); **g** flawless (24); **h** by rote (25); **i** articulated (29); **j** analogous (29); **k** components (33); **l** batches (47); **m** incentive (48); **n** paraphernalia (48)

Multiple choice

1 C (33–36); **2** A (16–21); **3** D (30–33); **4** A (47–50); **5** B (58); **6** C (60–65); **7** C (93–95);

Vocabulary items included in Vocabulary review

meet a need (4), mundane (4), uncanny (22), limb (30), components (33), batch (47), incentive (48), leap to a conclusion (51), dispense with (78)

▶Focus on writing 1 (p. 160)

Check that the topic and notes are clear to the students and remind them of the need to make notes before they begin. Remind them, too, that they won't have time during the exam to prepare both a rough version of the essay and a fair copy.

This would be a suitable topic for timed writing practice. Allow 40 minutes.

▶Text 3 (p. 161)

Optional pre-questions

1 What modern invention does the writer so object to? Why?

2 Which modern gadgets does the writer object to children having?

3 What change has occurred at the library? What does the writer most regret about it?

Suggested answers

1 The computer; because computers replace human beings in many situations and so make many everyday processes, like shopping or buying petrol, more impersonal. They also encourage us to rely on them to do our thinking for us.

2 Digital watches; computer toys; calculators.

3 Computers which give access to old manuscripts and newspaper cuttings have been installed; she can no longer actually handle the original documents.

Suggested answers to questions

1 Cleverly-designed piece of equipment.

2 An item whose effect spreads through your day and spoils it.

3 She doesn't seem to think it will be particularly effective because it involves several fiddly processes which take time and seem no more efficient than current procedures.

4 It's impersonal. There's little or no contact with people serving in shops or garages these days.

5 The old system before people were replaced by computers.

6 They don't help children to learn to tell the time.

7 An old-fashioned game.

8 Because it is a vocabulary which has no connection with literature. It expresses no feelings or perceptions.

9 They perform tasks which we used to do the hard way. They also encourage us to want the latest, most advanced model that will make our lives even easier.

10 The bright new screens which give access to the computer memory.

11 To plan to bring down the government by some cunning means.

12 originate from

13 Fantasies of computers taking over the world.

14 Because 15 years ago the idea of the computer as a machine did not exist in the dictionary. The machine has taken over from the man in that time.

15 Give marks for a well-expressed paragraph including the following points:

They make shopping impersonal and take away jobs; computer toys have replaced old-fashioned social games; digital watches stop children from learning to tell the time; computers teach an empty language and discourage expressive speaking; they encourage people to be lazy and acquisitive.

▶Language check (p. 162)

Dependent Prepositions 6: Preposition + Noun

on the basis that	**on** one's own
in business	**in** other words
by chance	**under** pressure
in/out of control of	**in** possession
at all costs	**at** present
in debt	**on** purpose
on fire	**in** use
on the one hand	**on** the whole

▶Focus on grammar (p. 162)

A brief review of the points about modal verbs which were covered in Unit 4 (p. 62) would be a useful introduction.

As in other Focus on grammar sections, students will be more actively involved if they suggest examples of their own to supplement those given in the book.

Exercise

a I should have finished; they will have to wait
b I was able to get hold of
c We didn't have to wait
d You could have done
e I must come to a decision
f I could see
g you have to fill in
h will you be able to deliver
i You (we) needn't have bought
j You could have given me a hand
k Need you/Do you really have to/Must you ask my advice
l You needn't make out
m I should/ought to book
n you should/ought to have thought

►Communication activity (p. 165)

(Allow 10–20 minutes for this activity).

Preparation

(Books closed)

1 Revise the language of describing objects which was practised in Part 2 of the Lead-in to this unit. Extend with additional objects/pictures, if necessary.

2 Read the description on page 165 and ask students to guess what it is. If they have difficulty, repeat sentence by sentence, at dictation speed, while students build up a drawing of the object (a needle). Check any new vocabulary.

3 Decide which students will work together and allot roles. It's best for weaker students to work with stronger ones for this activity.

(Books open)

4 Tell students to open their books on page 165 and read the general instructions. Check understanding. Students then turn to their respective lists.

5 (Optional) If there are a number of weaker students in the group, it would be helpful to let them have a 5 minute practice phase with stronger students (who have the same role), working in pairs. In this way they can acquire the necessary vocabulary for the task.

6 Organise seating in such a way that there is no possibility of one student seeing his/her partner's list. This can be *either* face to face, *or* back to back.

Pair work

1 Check that the 'rules' are being obeyed: ie that not too much is given away; that the right sort of questions are being asked; and that scoring is correct.
2 Note errors and language gaps unobtrusively.

Feedback

1 Discuss results and any particular difficulties experienced.
2 Focus on errors and language gaps noted.

►Focus on listening (p. 165)

1 *(Books closed)* Ask what 'the world's most valuable mineral' is. Discuss.
(Books open) Scan questions for answer.

2 Emphasise that the topic is dealt with from a general knowledge, rather than a purely scientific point of view.

3 Pair work, followed by feedback. It's obviously important not to confirm or deny any suggested answers at this point.

4 Listening task

Answers:

a To distinguish it from the many other chemical compounds which are also classed as salts.
b Because of its importance to the health of man and his animals, and also for industry.
c 3 per cent.
d It's spread on the roads in order to thaw (melt) ice and snow in winter.
e in Ethiopia
f rock salt; brine (sea water)
g The Dead Sea of Jordan; The Great Salt Lake of the USA.
h a shallow pool constructed beside the sea or an estuary, from which salt is collected.
i By mining or by being forced out of the ground as brine.
j To keep the salt running freely.

Vocabulary items included in Vocabulary review

by no means; deficiency; thaw; commodity; bulk; ancestor.

►Focus on register (p. 166)

1 C; 2 C; 3 D; 4 D; 5 A

Vocabulary items included in Vocabulary review

augment; stringent.

►Focus on writing 2 (p. 167)

Discuss the notes for this task and revise and extend topic vocabulary. If the essay is set for homework, advise students to set themselves a time limit of forty minutes and, of course, to make notes!

►Focus on listening (p. 168)

Part 1

concentration beds	F	level of spring tide	A
lock	E	crystallisation bed	G
storage pond inlet	C	normal high tide	Ba
storage pond	D		

If the normal salt content of sea water is taken as approximately 3%, the salt content of the brine reaching the crystallisation beds is 24%.

Part 2

2 cleaning and renovation of salterns
1 removal of water from tops of beds
5 piling of salt between beds
... ~~smoothing and beating of salt~~
3 preconcentration period
6 piling of salt on the edges of ponds
... ~~drainage of water through bottom of beds~~
4 harvesting of salt

▶**Vocabulary practice** (p. 169)

Review

1	B (2.4)	8	B (1.15)	14	A (L 1)	20	A (3.27)
2	D (2.4)	9	A (2.47)	15	D (L 1)	21	A (3.24)
3	C (2.58)	10	C (2.51)	16	C (L 1)	22	B (2.49)
4	A (2.30)	11	C (L 1)	17	A (3.12)	23	C (3.35)
5	B (2.22)	12	D (L 1)	18	D (3.42)	24	B (R)
6	D (2.78)	13	B (L 1)	19	B (3.38)	25	D (R)
7	C (2.33)						

Phrasal verbs: SET

1 set in; **2** set out; **3** set the dog on; **4** set about; **5** set off; **6** set to; **7** set me off; **8** set up; **9** set off; **10** set out

The prefix 'out-'

1 outstay; **2** outwit; **3** outclassed; **4** outweighs; **5** outmanoeuvred; **6** outshone; **7** outnumbered; **8** outlived; **9** outdone

▶**Grammar practice** (p. 172)

1 (1) take; (2) but/yet; (3) affect/influence; (4) lives; (5) which; (6) what; (7) actually; (8) should; (9) press/push; (10) give; (11) make; (12) Throughout; (13) dependent/reliant; (14) level; (15) has; (16) ancestors/(grand)parents/forebears; (17) disease; (18) majority; (19) on; (20) unable

2 *a* long as you bring; *b* of being; *c* have/have found out/have known; *d* had taken; *e* of whom; *f* being met; *g* had it; *h* must have been waiting; *i* what date/day it was/what the date was/the date; *j* no good/use trying to

UNIT **10** The Consumer Society

▶**Summary of Contents**

▶**Lead-in** (p. 173)

First advert

1 An image combining luxury and good-living; success and sophistication; comfort, security, warmth and domesticity.

2 The books in the bookcase, the elegantly framed oil paintings of horses on the walls, the antique sofa, table and brass log basket, the silver tray and crystal decanter (suggesting education, culture and good taste); the two people's clothes, the labrador (gun-dog) and the tasteful decor (suggesting a certain social class with a traditional, country lifestyle). In addition, the inset in the top right hand corner suggests that the woman manages the household economy while her husband earns a living. In the picture, he seems to be congratulating her on her good sense in buying the stove.

3 It's likely to be aimed at the middle classes – at the professional and business people who own their own homes and could afford to buy and install a fire like this. These would probably be people in their thirties or forties who identify with the people and lifestyle represented in the picture, or who aspire to be like them and live as they do.

4 eg expensive clothes for men and women, perfume and after-shave, whisky, brandy etc.

Second advert

1 This scene is distinctly *ordinary* by comparison with the first. It looks like a typical surburban kitchen with its brightly patterned wallpaper and its functional units. Various items in the picture suggest that it is in daily use rather than just a specially designed glamorous setting for an advertisement. We can see, for example, a shopping basket, in the bottom right hand corner, and on the work surfaces, a tea towel, colander, packet of breakfast cereal, tea pot, toaster and so on. Mr Sinclair, too, is hardly the glamorous stereotype normally associated with advertising!

2 The main appeal is one of humour. We look from the picture to the caption and then our eye returns to the picture with amused surprise when we realise what is referred to by 'Mrs Sinclair's old dishwasher'.

3 The style is informal, with a number of colloquial expressions such as 'nigh on', and 'without so much as a murmur'. The copy continues the joke of the caption and picture and invites one to read further. Sentence and paragraphs are short and easy to read, and the use of direct speech adds to the informality and makes the copy more lively.

Instead of proclaiming the machine's advantages, the advertiser uses the comments of a 'satisfied customer' to suggest them, in a more subtle and persuasive way. Mr Sinclair's arguments for treating the machine as a necessity rather than as a luxury are made to seem particulary sensible and convincing.

4 *The facts:*
It takes pots and pans as well as crockery and cutlery. There is no need to rinse items beforehand.

Suggested:
It has a large capacity. (Who knows how much the Sinclairs' 'whole day's washing up' is?)
The machine is reliable.
After sales service will be prompt and efficient.

Pairwork

1 *a* eg cleanness/brightness; efficient housekeeping; good, caring motherhood
  b eg hygiene; health; freshness; scientific respectability
  c eg relaxation, satisfaction, sophistication
  d eg technical sophistication

2 eg special offers; free gifts; price cuts; attractive packaging etc.

▶Text 1 (p. 175)

Optional pre-questions

Para 1   What factors led to the development of advertising on a national basis and to the brand-naming of goods?
Para 2   What change did the economic depression of 1873–94 bring about in the way small businesses operated?
Para 3   What changes took place in the soap trade during the second half of the 19th Century?
Para 4   What happened to firms which didn't advertise their products?

Suggested answers

1 The introduction of large scale factory production and the development of new products.

2 It caused them to combine together to form larger units producing a wider range of goods, and to rely increasingly on advertising as a way of creating a market for their goods.

3 At first there were a great many small manufacturers producing unnamed bars of soap, but later a number of leading companies took control of the market by using aggressive selling techniques, including the branding of their soap to make it more recognisable.

4 They ran into financial difficulties or were taken over by larger companies.

Multiple choice

1 B (3); 2 D (6–9); 3 A (15–19); 4 B (32–33); 5 D (38–39); 6 C (36–37, 43–44)

Vocabulary items included in Vocabulary review

get into full swing (3), to weather, a slump (17), take steps to (19), usher in (20), slogan (36), as distinct from (43), campaign, to mount (45).

▶Gimmicks (p. 176)

This topic forms a lead-in to Text 2.
Ask students to think specific examples of gimmicks they've seen, and encourage a general discussion about advertising incentives and their effectiveness.

▶Text 2 (p. 177)

Pre-questions Suggested answers

1 It offers new school equipment for children in exchange for labels from cans of baked beans.

2 The offer concerns school facilities which are normally the responsibility of government rather than private enterprise.

3 She seems to be worried about the implications of the new campaign.

Vocabulary matching

a pox (6); b gist (7); c soft sell (7/8); d aftermath (9); e concern (33); f tight spots (34); g plugging (39); h full-blown (42); i clout (53)

Multiple choice

1 B; 2 B (9/10) 3 D (20/24) 4 A (49–53); 5 C (68–76)

Vocabulary items included in Vocabulary review

implications (17), mask (22), shift in (45), pressed for (70), deprived (74).

▶Focus on writing 1 (p. 178)

Either set topic as timed essay practice, *or* prepare the ground beforehand by:

1 reviewing the advertising methods which have been touched on already in this unit and eliciting futher examples, to be listed on board.

2 discussing possible danger areas, with specific examples, eg:
  a the cigarette advertisement that associates smoking with masculinity and could influence teenage boys to start smoking.
  b the advertisement for an expensive toy which is aimed directly at children and may lead them to exert unfair pressure on their hard-up parents to buy it.

3 eliciting suggestions about, and discussing, possible controls.

►Text 3 (p. 179)

Part 1 – pre-questions Suggested answers

a Because there has been too much fishing in international waters in recent times and, as a result, the numbers of fish caught are likely to decrease by 20% in the near future.
b Because it could be used in the same way as cod, the most common fish used in the important fishfinger industry.
c Not at all.
d Because reporters discovered that the fish had the unattractive name of rats-tail and they published this in the papers. As a result of the negative public reaction, the main fishfinger producer then abandoned the idea of using the new fish.

Part 2 – pre-questions Suggested answers

a Effective advertising
b By creating excitement about a product.
c Margarine.

Suggested answers to questions

1 anxiety/fear

2 increasing productivity (larger and more frequent crops, rearing more young animals) by interfering with natural processes.

3 We are able to exploit a large range of natural resources, including ones which have traditionally been ignored.

4 To avoid a dispute with another country over fishing rights.

5 was suitable for

6 To find out people's reaction to something.

7 They have few scruples about what they put into their products and are only influenced by what they think the consumers will accept.

8 Because all the money spent on research had been wasted.

9 They were afraid that consumers might think the product contained the fish called rats-tail, and not buy it.

10 They choose only traditional foods which they are familiar with.

11 Because it doesn't sound at all appetising and, of course, it was a completely new food product.

12 It refers to the work of the advertisers.

13 It refers to advertising the novelty of a food product.

14 He must have been horrified because he was a bird lover and the book dealt with the cooking of songbirds.

15 Give marks for a well-expressed paragraph, without irrelevant detail, and including the following points: Attitudes as to what's acceptable and what's not vary considerably from person to person and from country to country; most people are very conservative in their choice of food, preferring traditional, familiar items; result of upbringing, religion or personal preference; new food products induce anxiety; to overcome this they must appear in familiar forms and must have acceptable names; effective advertising is crucial in influencing public attitudes to food.

Vocabulary items included in Vocabulary review

fiddle with (25), species (35), hug (38), come up with (39), lend itself to (44), sound out (49), illusion (133)

►Focus on grammar (p. 182)

Exercise 1

a She explained that he had gone out at 10 o'clock the previous morning and that nobody had seen him since then.
b She cried that she didn't know what to do, adding/explaining that the news had come as a complete shock.
c She told me that there was nothing on at the cinema (just) then/at that time that she wanted to see and added that the last time she had been to the cinema had been two years before.
d He told me to phone him the following Sunday when he hoped to have more information./explaining that he hoped to have more information by then.
e She said that she'd stay (there) by the 'phone for the next ten minutes in case they called again./as they might call again./explaining that they might call again.

Exercise 2

a They told me that I might catch the 6 o'clock train if I hurried.
b I explained that I couldn't have a small dog as a pet because my flat was too small.
c She exclaimed that I must be exhausted as I hadn't had a break all day.
d He told me that I ought to ask for a pay rise since I'd brought the company a lot of business./adding that I'd brought the company a lot of business.
e She said she hadn't needed to pack a suitcase as she was only going for the day.
f He told us that we needn't have waited up for him as/explaining that he was quite capable of letting himself in.
g He said he'd rather I didn't tell anyone what he'd just told me.
h She explained that she might be able to give me a lift but that she wouldn't know until the morning.
i He told the policeman that he couldn't find his door key, explaining that that was why he had broken the window.
j They told us that she should be delighted when she heard the news.
k He told me that I must always ask for a receipt when I paid by cash.
i He said if he could help me he would, but added that he wasn't in a position to do so at that moment.

Exercise 3

a Our hostess invited us to sit down and make ourselves at home.
b My friend warned me not to touch the Record button since I could erase the tape.
c My brother urged me to take the matter up with my solicitor, adding that it could be very serious.
d She advised me to pay a visit to the Citizen's Advice Bureau, saying that they would be able to tell me what my rights were.
e They recommended us to try the squid, which was delicious (they said), if we were eating at Mario's.
f The teacher forbade us to use a dictionary during the test.

g My aunt begged me not to forget to let her know when we'd arrived safely, adding that she'd be worried to death unless we did.

h The two visitors asked if they could come in.

i The man suggested that we should try the corner shop, explaining that they sometimes stayed open late on Sundays.

j He encouraged me to enter the exam, pointing out that I had nothing to lose and that it would be good experience for me.

▶ Communication activity (p. 186)

(Allow about 20 mins for this activity)

Introduction

Introduce the topic by asking students what they would do if they found that something they had bought was faulty – eg an alarm clock which doesn't ring. Describe briefly consumers' rights in the UK under the Trade Description Act, and discuss how far consumers are protected in the students' own countries.

Preteach 'breach' as a verb and as a noun, (students may remember it occurring in the 'Neighbours' text in Unit 4 and in the Vocabulary review section of that unit) and 'loophole'.

Pairwork

Little monitoring needed but be on hand to help with queries as to vocabulary: eg 'upstanding' (Situation 7), 'rubble' (Situation 10).

Feedback

It may be best to ask only one student to turn to the key on page 199, to supply the answers, or for the teacher to take this role.

In any case, the situations should be discussed generally beforehand and the problems illustrated in Situations 2, 4 and 10 can be described more fully.

▶ Focus on listening (p. 187)

1

ITEM	1	2	3
COMPLAINT FROM	Mrs Stewart	Mrs Bowen	Mr Walters
CONSUMER AREA	MO	SR	MO
GOODS CONCERNED	pushchairs etc	suit	stamps
PROBLEM	a b	g	d
AMOUNT PAID	£615	£90	x

2 B; **3** D; **4** C; **5** A; **6** C; **7** D; **8** B

Lexis

Case 1: the tip of an iceberg, the upshot, to fork out (slang), shoddy, to cut a long story short, on behalf of, to get the ball rolling, flimsy, none too solid, con-man, premises, fall foul, to con, elusive.

Case 2: to be taken to the cleaners (slang), shrink, assertion, peremptory.

Case 3: inexcusable, issue/serve a summons, adverse, unsolicited, harassment, humiliate.

▶ Language Check (p. 188)

Prefixes

2 a– without; **ab–** from/away from; **ad–** to/towards; **anti–** opposed to/against; **co–/com–/con–** with/together; **mis–/mal–** bad/wrong; **pro–** supporting/in favour of; **syn–/sym–** sharing (with)/together; **uni–** one/the same.

3 a) to **disband:** to stop operating as a single group
b) to **synchronize:** to do at the same time and speed; (of watches) to adjust so that they show exactly the same time
c) to **malfunction:** to fail to work properly
d) **anti-clockwise:** moving in the opposite direction to the direction in which the hands of a clock move
e) **asymetrical:** with two sides or halves that are different in shape, size or style
f) a **propensity:** a natural tendency to behave in a particular way
g) to **coincide;** to happen at or around the same time
h) to **abstain:** to deliberately not do something
i) **adjoining:** next to
j) in **unison:** together/at the same time

▶ Focus on register (p. 189)

1 B (Maintenance) **2 D** (Durability) **3 B** (Enjoyment time + Satisfaction) **4 A** (irreplaceability) **5 D** (Vet's fees) **6 C** (Children outgrow them) **7 B** (infections such as salmonella) **8 C** (something to gnaw on)

Vocabulary items included in Vocabulary review

outgrow; gnaw (Rabbits).

▶ Focus on writing 2 (p. 190)

a They seem more applicable to manufactured items such as cars or vacuum cleaners than to living animals. Pets are treated in exactly the same way as other consumer purchases and the effect is intentionally humorous.

b Maintenance: time spent looking after the animal (cleaning, grooming, etc.).
Enjoyment time: time during which owners actively enjoyed the company of their pets, by playing with them, etc.
Durability: the expected life-span of the animal.

c eg *Price:* How much did your pet cost?/How much did you pay for your pet?
Running costs: How much does it cost you a week to keep your pet?
Maintenance: How much time do you spend a day looking after your pet?
Enjoyment time: How much time each day do you spend actively enjoying your pet?
Durability: How long do x's live, on average?
Satisfaction: How satisfied would you say your were with your pet? Would you buy another? Why? Why not?

Go through the notes orally and remind students once again of the need to make notes, plan structure, and frame composition with an effective introduction and conclusion.

▶ Vocabulary practice (p. 191)

Review

1 B (1.17)	**8 A** (1.43)	**14 B** (2.74)	**20 B** (3.25)
2 D (1.3)	**9 C** (1.36)	**15 B** (2.66)	**21 C** (2.17)
3 A (1.45)	**10 D** (3.38)	**16 C** (2.45)	**22 D** (3.49)
4 A (1.17)	**11 A** (3.35)	**17 B** (2.40)	**23 B** (3.133)
5 C (1.19)	**12 B** (R)	**18 A** (2.22)	**24 A** (3.44)
6 B (1.20)	**13 C** (2.70)	**19 C** (3.39)	**25 D** (R)
7 D (1.45)			

Phrasal verbs: COME

1 came in for; **2** come by; **3** come round to; **4** came into; **5** came at; **6** came out; **7** came up with; **8** came across; **9** come about; **10** came round; **11** came down with; **12** came across

▶Grammar practice (p. 194)

1 (1) drawing; (2) somebody/people; (3) word; (4) expense; (5) number; (6) usual/normal; (7) public; (8) put/place; (9) take/buy; (10) bring; (11) pass/spread; (12) go; (13) carry; (14) appear/talk/advertise; (15) organise/arrange; (16) content/satisfied; (17) leave; (18) add; (19) appealing; (20) where

2 *a* He apologised for not ringing (having rung) to say he'd be late.

b Tired though/as he was, he agreed to play tennis.

c I didn't realise the extent to which he was influenced by his brother.

d He denied telling (having told) anyone about my/our scheme.

e You oughtn't to have scared your mother like that.

f By the time the letter arrives, he's likely to have left (he'll probably have left).

g The last time the window cleaners called was at least six months ago.

h She demanded to know where on earth I/we had been all that time.

i Despite the (heavy) weight of the suitcase, he managed to lift it easily.

Exam Practice Listening

▶Home Improvements (p. 201)

Lead-in

1 Write up the title and ask students to work in pairs and make a list of examples of things people do to improve their homes. Suggest that they think about a range of improvements from simple and cheap to major and expensive, and about the outside as well as the inside. (5 mins)

2 Ask students to report back their ideas and discuss briefly. If you are not using the material specifically for exam practice, you may want to write ideas up and to check topic vocabulary at this stage.

3 Ask whether one person's idea of an "improvement" would always be seen as such by others. Can they think of examples?

Task

Either play the tape right through twice, pausing briefly at the end of each section, *or* repeat each section and check answers as you go along. Allow students time to read through the questions beforehand.

Part 1

plastic kitchen chairs		beige bath, sink, WC
an antique pine kitchen table ✓		floral wallpaper
an old-fashioned cooker ✓		plain pale blue tiles ✓
a traditional bath		

Part 2

	Adds Value	No Effect	Easier to Sell	Harder to Sell
Inside				
gold taps		✓		
loft conversion	✓			
downstairs WC			✓	
kitchen/dining room	✓			
fitted cupboards			✓	
carpets + curtains			✓	
Outside				
swimming pool		✓		
conservatory	✓			
climbing plants				✓
fountains		✓		
fast-growing trees				✓

Part 3

a T   *b* T   *c* F   *d* T   *e* F   *f* F

▶ Time is Money (p. 202)

Lead-in

Ask students how many devices for telling the time they can think of. Check topic vocabulary eg sundial, hourglass, wristwatch, grandfather clock etc; hands, face, case, winder, pendulum etc; gain/lose time etc.

Task

Allow students time to read through the questions.

1 See opposite
2 C
3 D (*the damp sets in*)
4 C (*. . . show me the ropes*)
5 A
6 B (*. . . people regard their clocks as people*)
7 B
8 D (*not very lucrative*)

1

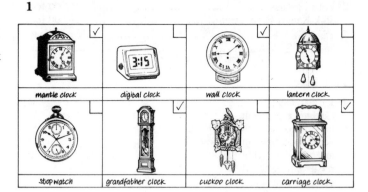

mantle clock · digital clock · wall clock · lantern clock
stop watch · grandfather clock · cuckoo clock · carriage clock

---

▶ Himalayan Kingdoms (p. 203)

Lead-in

1 Ask students to look at the photograph. Now students can make a list of words (nouns, adjectives, verbs) which come to mind when they think about such a mountain (3 mins). (Encourage them to think of words expressing emotional responses as well as purely descriptive terms.)

2 Ask students to compare their lists and then write up three headings on the board: **positive, neutral, negative**. As students give you their words, ask the class to decide which heading they belong to.

3 Discuss briefly any experience students may have of mountain activities such as skiing or climbing. Find out how many would be interested in going on a package holiday to the Himalayas and their reasons why or why not.

Task

You are advised to repeat each section and check answers as you go along. Allow time for students to read through the questions.

Part One

1 from 15 to 60+
2 over 60
3 *b* the number of consecutive days' trekking
4 14 − 15,000 feet
5 headaches

Part Two

1 See map below.

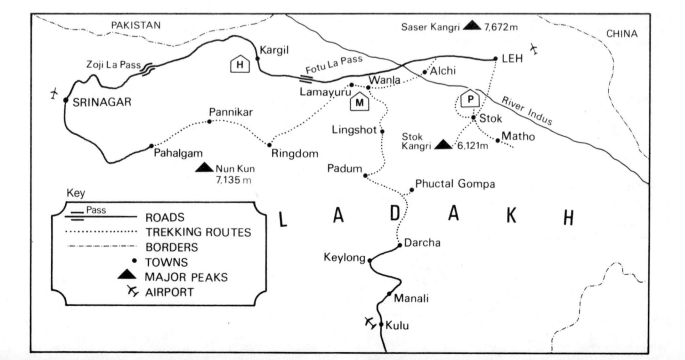

2 Fotu La Pass.. 14,500 feet
  Stok Kangri Base Camp .... 17,500 feet
3 climb Stok Kangri .... 7 hours
  descend Stok Kangri................................... 3 hours

Part Three

1 local transport   ✓
   climbing equipment   ✓
   hotel accommodation in Delhi   ✓
   accommodation during the trek   ✓
   international flights   ✓
   meals during the trek   ☐
   camping equipment   ✓
   dinners in Delhi   ☐

2

Indian airport tax	£5.00
INSURANCE	£41·00
Indian visa	£20.00
SPENDING MONEY	£5 a day

3 (Saturday) 6th August to (Saturday) 27th August
4 2 months in advance

▶ A Many-Sided Therapy (p. 205)

Lead-in

1 Ask students who they could go to, apart from a doctor, if they had a health problem. Elicit such terms as herbalist, faith healer, chiropractor, osteopath and acupuncturist, and explore students' views on these alternative therapies together with any experience they may have had of such treatment.

  NB Don't single out osteopathy for special attention since this would give the game away as far as question 2 is concerned!

2 If this is not an exam practice session, allow students to study the two diagrams and to check the relevant vocabulary in pairs.

Task

Either play the whole recording through twice, allowing a brief pause after Part 1, *or* repeat each section and check answers as you along. Allow time for students to read through the questions.

Part 1

1
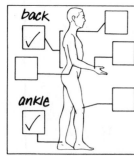
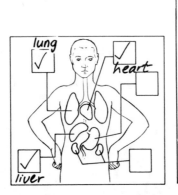

2 c   3 b   4 d   5 c   6 a

Part Two

  1 T
  2 F (in my early teens)
  3 F (I used to be in the rugby scrum. . .)
  4 T (a fairly constant, nagging ache)
  5 F (I just let it ride)
  6 T
  7 T (a slightly hunched position)
  8 F (. . . lower right hand side, but it aches across)
  9 F (a stiff neck)
10 T (slip your things off)

▶ Another Crime Statistic (p. 206)

Lead-in

1 Ask whether students have ever had anything stolen from them, perhaps on holiday or as the result of a burglary. If a number of students have, then ask them to swap stories in pairs or small groups. (3–5 mins)

2 Ask students to report back to the class on what *another* student told them. Discuss what can be done after a crime of this kind, and how such crimes can be prevented.

  NB There should be no need to check the names of the pieces of furniture in question 1!

Task

You will probably find it best to replay each section and check answers as you go along. Allow time for students to read through the questions.

Part 1

1 C

2 earrings, (watches)

3 a brooch

4 petty cash, cheque book and credit card

5 hi-fi system   ✓
   radio   ?
   video   x
   TV   ✓
   camera   ?
   personal computer   x
   microwave oven   x
   savings account book   ?
   car   ✓

Part 2

1 Check the meaning of "aggrieved" and "premises".

WESSEX CONSTABULARY

CRIME REPORT / REGISTER

1. Offence *Domestic Burglary*
2. To whom reported *Redfield Police Station*
3. Time reported *11.30 am* .... Date reported *7 May*
4. Name of aggrieved person *CLARK Anna Jane (MS)*
   Date of birth *31.5.54*
5. Address *36 Acton Road, Redfield*
   Telephone number *426700*
6. Time of offence *Between 10 and 11.15 am*
   Place of offence *at above address*
7. Type of premises *flat*
8. Means of entry to premises *door forced open*
9. Property stolen *brooch* .... Value *£50*
   Description of property stolen *oval shape, glass, antique*
10. Officer attending scene *P.C. West* .... number *1690*

2 A (Door at the side; trees at the back; bedroom looking on to the road)

Part Three

a F (this type's not particularly secure)
b T (A similar thing happened last year. . .)
c F
d F (I'll try and get someone today *-ie someone to mend the door*)
e T (You'd disturbed things and I don't think they'd *-ie the finger print people-* be able to get much.)
f F (they're purely opportunist)
g F (someone who bears you a grudge for some reason)

▶Acquiring New Skills (p. 208)

Lead-in

1 Write the letters D.I.Y. on the board, check the meaning, and ask students in pairs to make a list of the kinds of jobs that a D.I.Y. enthusiast might undertake.

2 Get students to report back their ideas and find out if anyone has any experience of such work. Discuss the attraction of D.I.Y. and ask what jobs they think would *not* be suitable for D.I.Y. enthusiasts and why. Raise the question of whether D.I.Y. appeals to women and why/why not.

Task

If your students are reasonably close to exam standard, it would probably be best to play the whole recording through twice, pausing briefly after each section. If they need more help, repeat each section and check answers as you go along. You may also want to check through the jobs shown in the pictures which are as follows:

a changing a plug, **b** laying a carpet, **c** putting up shelves, **d** using an electric drill to drill into a wall, **e** wallpapering,

f using a blowtorch to mend a burst pipe, **g** taking a switch apart and mending it, **h** making soft furnishings (eg curtains), **i** fitting a lock (eg a mortice lock), **j** glazing (eg replacing a window), **k** bricklaying, **l** tiling a bathroom.

Allow time for students to read through the questions.

Part One

1 C   **2** B

Part Two

1 c, d, f, g, i, j, l
2 *a* f (quite terrifying) and j (nerve-racking)
  b l (. . . I'd always thought was an incredibly difficult thing to do.)
  c f (you'd save huge amounts of money)

Part Three

	Course	Additional Information
1	*car maintenance*	*8 days*
2	*computer course*	runs at a different centre
3	*woodwork and carving*	—

▶Your Friendly Local Radio Station (p. 210)

Lead-in

Introduce the topic of *national* versus *local* radio and TV: what are the differences of content and style? What can local radio and TV do that the national media cannot? What time of day would local programmes be most popular?

Ask students to comment on local radio or TV programmes that they know. Which features have they enjoyed/found useful? Which aspects do they dislike? (If students don't have this experience, ask them to say what they would most *like* to be included in a local programme for their area.)

Task

Allow time for students to read through the questions and check that they know what to do for question 1 particularly.

1

Which did you hear?		Which did you hear someone mention?	
time check	✓	weather reports	✓
daily recipe		record requests	
competition		public transport information	✓
health advice		local news	✓
gardening advice		world news	✓
birthday greetings		crime report	
sports information	✓	traffic information	✓

2 C (. . . more resources away from administration and behind the microphone)

3 thirteen minutes to eight (7.47)

4 speech

5 two

6 only 8 or 9 miles apart

7 2 or 3 minutes

8 C (we're into our stride earlier than anyone else)

9 A (I haven't got much to say to people who work with us and who help produce the programme.)

10 C (. . . talk to yourself in a room for three hours with nobody laughing at what you say except yourself – the only way to survive. . .)

▶ Something to Complain About (p. 211)

Lead-in

1 Ask if anyone has ever had to complain about something they've bought. If a number of students have, ask them to swap stories in pairs or small groups. (3–5 mins)

2 Ask students to report back to the class on what *another* student has told them. Discuss the best way of complaining – in person, in writing, or by telephone – and what the important things to bear in mind are (eg keep receipts and copies of correspondence, insist on your rights etc.).

NB There should be no need to check the names of the items in question 1!

Task

Allow time for students to read through the questions.

1 C

2 B (gauge at bottom, L-shaped plastic piece)

3 D (a month out of guarantee)

4 C

5

	√	#
She wrote to the manufacturers	✓	5
She spoke to the manager in the shop	✓	3
The manufacturers sent her a form to fill in	✗	
She contacted the shop's head office	✗	
She spoke to an assistant in the shop	✓	2
She telephoned the manufacturers	✓	7
She went to the shop where she had bought the equipment	✓	1
The local agents replaced the equipment	✗	
She sent the manufacturers' letter back to them	✓	8
The manufacturers sent her letter back to her	✓	6
The equipment was repaired free of charge	✓	9
She spoke to the manager on the telephone	✓	4

6 B

Exam Practice Interview (p. 212)

The six oral 'packages' in this section are linked to topics in the book and can either be introduced gradually, as students work through the book, or reserved for intensive practice when the ten units have been completed.

The packages may be used for guided examination preparation or as practice tests under examination conditions.

Examination procedure

1 Group or individual?

It is now possible for examination centres to choose *either* the usual candidate/examiner format for the Interview *or* to have groups of two or three candidates with an examiner. The advantage of the group option is that it allows for more natural and realistic communication, and for this reason it is strongly advocated by the U.C.L.E.S. language advisors. This kind of communication will be extremely familiar to students who have participated in the communication activities in this book.

Note: If your local centre is unable, for practical reasons, to offer the group option, there are still a number of advantages in conducting some of the practice tests in groups:

– students will co-operate, learning from each other's strengths.

– more communication will be generated.

– the experience will be less isolating and more confidence-building.

2 Optional background reading

Candidates may choose to discuss one of three sets texts as the basis for Section C in the Interview. Since these texts vary from year to year, it is not possible to include example questions in this practice material. An up-to-date list of set texts is included in the current Regulations published by the University of Cambridge Local Examinations Syndicate.

3 Interview sections

The examiner's material consists of a number of theme-based sets of photographs and other prompts. The interview is in three sections, as in the Cambridge First Certificate exam, and the main differences between the two examinations is that Proficiency candidates are expected to be able to produce longer stretches of clear, coherent speech and to discuss more serious or complex issues.

Section 1: Picture Conversation

The examiner asks questions about a photograph and leads on to more general discussion of related themes. In a group interview candidates may also be required to ask questions themselves.

Section 2: Reading Passages

One or more short passages are used as the basis for a discussion between the examiner and the candidate, or between candidates. Reading aloud is no longer required, although candidates may quote from the texts to illustrate their comments.

Section 3: Structured communication activity

A wide range of activities based on pictures, diagrams or texts is used. These may include advertisements, timetables, weather reports, questionnaires, maps, etc. Candidates may be required to take part in a role play, solve a problem or discuss opinions. They may also choose to discuss a set book during this section.

4 Marking

The three sections of the Interview are assessed **as a whole** on six scales, each of 0–5 marks. The scales are as follows:

Fluency
Grammatical accuracy
Pronunciation: prosodic features (stress, rhythm, etc)
Pronunciation: individual sounds
Communicative ability
Vocabulary

Note: Marks scored in Paper 4 (Listening comprehension) and Paper 5 (Interview) together now account for one-third of the total marks in the examination.

Examination preparation

Section 1: Picture conversation

It is important to point out to students that the picture itself merely serves as a jumping-off point for conversation. The Interview is not a test of general knowledge but of the language skills listed in the previous section.

If it is not clear what is shown in a picture, or if a question is difficult to answer, it is perfectly valid to say so! What matters is to give the examiner sufficient opportunity to assess a candidate's English. This means giving full answers and illustrating remarks with examples where appropriate.

If students will be having the Interview in a group, they should also be given the opportunity to practise asking each other questions about these and other pictures.

Recommended procedures

Groupwork: students working together to answer the questions given, pooling ideas and vocabulary.
'Mock' interviews: students in pairs, one acting as 'examiner'.
'Mock' interviews: teacher and student(s).

Section 2: Reading passages

Again point out to students that this is not a test of reading comprehension. It is the way that they express their reactions to the passages, in English, that will be assessed. Reassure them that they will be given enough time to read through the passages and that, if there is a word or phrase they really don't understand, they should feel free to say so.
The candidate may be asked:
– what the source of a passage might be
– what the intention of the writer/speaker might have been
– what relation there is between the passage and the general theme of the discussion

Students need to be trained to look for clues in the text which give an indication as to the source and the writer's intention (whether it's a factual account or a persuasive piece of writing, for example). Encourage students to illustrate their comments by quoting briefly from the text.

Recommended procedures

Students read passages individually and then discuss their ideas about them with a partner. After that, **either** pairs team up to form groups of four. They then compare their conclusions, **or** pairs split up and new pairs are formed for further discussion.
'Mock' interviews: students read passages individually and then discuss their reactions individually or in groups with the teacher.
Note: If the students are weak in this aspect of the examination, it is helpful if the teacher designs focus questions for the first one or two practice sessions. These can be simple gist comprehension questions, or they can draw students' attention to key features in the passages.

Section 3: Structured communication activity

Point out how important it is to read the instructions carefully before beginning. After that, a pair or group should check that everyone understands exactly what to do. If they need to discuss how to tackle a particular task, how to start, or who should take which part, that will generate perfectly valid communication. The language produced in *talking about* the activity is just as useful to the examiner in assessing candidates as the language used in *participating in* the activity.

For this reason, it's best to keep explanations to a minimum and to let students have practice in using the kind of transactional language needed to work things out. For example:
How shall we go about this?
Who's going to write the answers down?
I think we should move on to the next point now, don't you?

▶ Homes (p. 212)

Section 1

Contrasting images of housing (in Hong Kong): A crude shack in the foreground, with densely packed multi-storey blocks – perhaps government built – in the distance.

Section 2

a Advice to the inexperienced home handyman which probably goes on to list recommended tools. Despite one or two colloquial expressions, the overall style suggests that this is written English, probably from an article in a magazine or newspaper. (Discuss topic in relation to students' own experience.)
b A more specialist piece discussing the case for the refurbishment of old buildings rather than their demolition. Fairly formal style although the use of the expression 'you see' suggests that this is spoken English – probably from a lecture or talk. (Discuss topic in relation to students' own home country.)

Section 3

The task involves the expression of opinions and the negotiation of decisions in the pair or group. Students should draw or write the different items on the plan and be prepared to explain the thinking behind their final layout to other students and/or to the teacher.

▶ Work (p. 214)

Section 1

A sculptor working with a kind of wooden hammer or mallet and chisel to carve a stone statue, perhaps of a traditional figure or a god. He seems to be from a Far Eastern country, perhaps Thailand.

Section 2

a Description of a visit to a car assembly plant. Use of language suggests a professional writer, probably a journalist. (Discuss the nature of the work.)
b Personal account of an apprenticeship as a furniture restorer. Fairly informal style although sentence construction suggests written English. (Discuss the types of work where apprenticeships are common, the role of the apprentice, and the experience from the apprentice's point of view.)

Section 3

This is a discussion topic for two or three students. Suggest students discuss unknown vocabulary (eg forecourt attendant) beforehand, and allow them to ask questions if necessary. A feedback stage is useful and this should involve students reporting back not only on their own opinions but also on their partner's, and on the discussion as a whole.

▶ Tourist or Traveller? (p. 216)

Section 1

A hiker or climber standing on a ridge and surveying the view over a village in the valley below and towards the high mountains beyond. Perhaps in the Himalayas.

Section 2

a Personal account of a train journey across India. The way the writer expresses surprise at the sight of rain clouds suggests that this is an extended journey rather than a package holiday, and that s/he's a traveller rather than a tourist. (In fact the extract is an excerpt from Paul Theroux's book, *The Great Railway Bazaar*.) (Discuss the relative merits of train journeys and air travel, and any relevant experience students may have.)

b Discussion of the reason people take holidays. Formal use of language suggests an academic lecture or article in a specialist journal. (Discuss students' own reasons for taking holidays.)

Section 3

A discussion topic. Allow students time to read through the various precautions and tell them to discuss and, if necessary, ask about any vocabulary which they are not sure of (eg suspect – adj). Allow a few minutes for the first part of the task and then ask students to begin the second part. Again, it is useful if pairs can compare their results afterwards, and perhaps feed back briefly to the whole class.

▶ Relationships (p. 218)

Section 1

Computer dating advertisement.

Section 2

a Request for advice on a personal problem – probably from a letter to an 'agony aunt'. (Discuss the role of in-laws in the students' own culture and their ideas for a solution to the problem outlined here. Alternatively, discuss the question of the 'agony aunts', why so many people seem to seek their advice, how useful their advice is likely to be and whether the students can imagine writing such a letter themselves.)

b Brother's description of his sister and of his relationship with the female members of his family. Either spoken or from the written version of an interview. (Discuss the influence of brothers and sisters in students' own experience.)

Section 3

1/2 Allow students a short time to read through the ten categories and make their selections. Encourage them to discuss their interpretation of the various categories (and any vocabulary problems) as well as to exchange opinions as to the usefulness of the list.

3 This involves discussion and negotiation. Students probably won't have time to complete a list of items for column B but they should be prepared to report back to the class on those they decide on.

▶ Crime and Punishment (p. 220)

Section 1

Prisoners working in a graveyard, under the supervision of a warder.

Section 2

a Advice on ways in which householders can co-operate with their neighbours and with the police to prevent crime. Possibly a public information announcement, but more likely to have been taken from a crime prevention leaflet or advertisement. (Discuss the idea of 'Neighbourhood Watch' schemes, and the public image of the police in students' own countries.)

b Part of a talk on crime prevention, perhaps given by a police officer, in which the speaker is about to recommend simple measures to prevent the theft of personal items such as wallets. (Ask what measures might be recommended and discuss any personal experience of the theft of their belongings students might have.)

Section 3

Allow time for students to look at the two lists and discuss any unknown vocabulary. They can either make their own choices and then compare results, or work together to reach decisions. Clearly the punishment depends on the particular circumstances in several cases, but this is intended to be a valid part of the discussion.

▶ Science and Technology (p. 222)

Section 1

Typewriters abandoned in a rubbish skip, contrasted with pictures of an electronic circuit and a microchip. (Images from an advertisement for word processors.)

Section 2

a From the announcement of the introduction of a new product, an electric car. Probably spoken by a company spokesman at an official launch. (Discuss the advantages and limitations of electric cars, and possibly the distinction made between an electric vehicle and an electric car.)

b Part of an introduction to basic principles of chemistry for a non-specialist audience. Probably spoken. (Discuss methods used by teachers, lecturers and TV presenters of making complex issues accessible to a wide audience, and students' own reactions to them.)

Section 3

Allow students time to read through the introduction and to consider the information in the pie-chart before they begin the discussion. Emphasise that they must reach a decision as to where the job losses should occur within the time allowed (5–10 mins). It is helpful if students are asked to report back briefly on their decisions and their reasons.

COURSE TAPESCRIPTS

▶UNIT 1 Focus on listening (p. 15)

Well, if everyone's here, I think I'd better begin.

Today we're going to look at a completely different architectural tradition. The city of Sana'a is the capital of the Yemen Arab Republic. You can see where it is on the map I handed out. There in the southern corner of the Arabian peninsula. Sana'a is notable because it's one of the best preserved traditional types of Islamic city, with its medieval aspect and its traditional organisation.

The houses in Sana'a are particularly interesting. They have between 5 and 9 storeys and are usually occupied by a single family. The building techniques and decorations which are used are centuries old and this is because of the unchanging needs and habits of the inhabitants.

In order to get a clearer picture of the design and use of these buildings, we'll take one particular house as a model. You should have a plan of the ground floor and long section through the house. As you listen to what I have to say, I'd like you to match the letters on the plans to the parts and uses of the house which are listed alongside.

The lower levels of the house are built of stone and are whitewashed for protection against the heavy showers which fall in the rainy season. The upper walls are made of baked brick. The roofs, which are flat, are used by the women for washing and drying clothes.

The door from the street opens into an area where goods can be loaded and unloaded. Beyond that is the main entrance hall from which stairs lead to the upper floors. You can see the stairs marked on the far side of the ground floor plan. Flanking the entrance hall are stables for animals. Cattle, sheep, goats, mules and donkeys are kept and sometimes a horse. Water can be drawn from a well in one corner of the entrance hall and this is used for the animals as well as for residents of the house.

The stairs leading to the upper floors are made of stone. The flights are short and there are frequent landings so that the climb to the top of the house isn't too arduous!

Above the entrance hall there are no living rooms but a storage area for wheat, corn, millet, and other grain. Here the corn is also ground into flour in another room which overlooks the street.

The main living rooms are on the next floor and they are entered through a large lobby from the stairs. This lobby is closed from the stairs by a door with a wooden shutter which is decorated with fine carvings. I've got pictures of some examples if any of you would like to see them later.

Directly above the main living rooms is the reception room or, to give it its proper name, the diwan. This is used by both men and women for family celebrations such as births, weddings and so on. There's also a lavatory-bathroom on this floor – the entrance is from the lobby on this floor.

Above the diwan and two floors above the living rooms are the smaller personal rooms used by the women and children, and the main cooking area with its simple stove and bench for preparing food. The position of the kitchen enables the women to be kept in seclusion and also prevents smoke from entering the living room.

There's a flat roof over the kitchen and this is where clothes are washed and dried, as I mentioned earlier.

Above the kitchen is the room where the women's clothes are kept and, at the top of the house, a long room called the mafraj. This has windows on three sides which give extensive views over the housetops. It's the principal room for entertaining guests and contains the family's finest possessions.

Now, I'd like to talk in a little more detail about construction methods . . . FADE

▶Unit 2 Focus on listening (p. 32)

I = Interviewer   A = Applicant

I Come in!

A Mr Sanderson? I hope. . .

I Yes, come in. You must be. . . (pause). . . Miss Jones.

A Yes, I am – Rosemary Jones. I hope I haven't kept you waiting.

I No, not at all – you're right on time, by my watch, at least. Do sit down. . . Now, let me see. . . I've got your application form somewhere here. . . (noise of paper rustling)
Yes! Here we are – Rosemary Jones. And you live at 12 Regent Street, Stanmore, is that right?

A Yes, that's right. It's my parents' address, actually. I'm looking for a bedsit somewhere nearer the centre of town at the moment.

I Good, yes, commuting can be a bit of a problem, can't it? And the cost of season tickets has just gone up again, but I mustn't get on to the subject of London Transport – it's something I have strong feelings about! Now. . . age. . . I see that you're twenty five.

A No, sorry, twenty three. It must be my writing!

I Right, I've got that. . . and you took English, French and Spanish A levels. Languages can obviously be very useful in this work. How do you reckon you speak your French now, for example?

A Well, I spent nine months in France after I left school, but . . .

I Oh yes, very nice, and what were you doing there?

A I was working as an au-pair with a family in Bordeaux. But I didn't get that much practice, I'm afraid, because both the husband and wife spoke English rather well and the baby was only seven months old! To be honest, my French is really pretty rusty now, though I'm sure it would come back to me with practice.

I Mm. . . and how about your Spanish?

A I'm virtually bi-lingual in Spanish, actually. You see, my mother is half Spanish and we usually go to see our relatives in Madrid every year or so.

I Good. And finally, your German?

A Well, that's roughly on a par with my French. They could both do with a bit of brushing up!

I Fine – now what have you been doing since you came back from France?

A Well, I've been working in a department store, selling perfume and cosmetics, and helping with the odd bit of translation for foreign customers.

I And what about your plans for the future?

A I've decided that what I'd really like to do is to go into the tourist industry.

I Why the tourist industry?

A Well, I love travel and I enjoy meeting people and. . .

I (interrupting) You're thinking of becoming a courier?

A Yes, to begin with, and then perhaps I could go into the admin side.

I I see, and you think you'd get to know the ropes with this job. But it isn't all plain sailing – I think it's only fair to point out that some people can be very awkward – especially when they're suffering from jet lag and the coach to take them to their hotels hasn't turned up. How do you think you'd cope under that sort of pressure?

A I should think it's all part of the job. You have to take the rough with the smooth in any job, don't you? Actually, I think I'd quite enjoy the challenge. You'd have to keep calm – and explain the reason behind the delay. I don't think people mind so much if they're kept in the picture.

I That all sounds very sensible. Still, don't be surprised when it does happen to you – (quickly) if you get the job, that is. Now, I ought to check on your general state of health. How would you assess it?

A I would say I'm fighting fit! I play squash twice a week, at least and I usually win! I don't smoke and I can't remember the last time I had to go to bed with 'flu or a cold.
I So you play squash, do you. . . (pause). . . And can you tell me about any other hobbies you have?
A Well, I'm keen on drama, of course, and I do like to see well-made films – I wouldn't go to see rubbish. I'm not a great music fan. . . Oh and I belong to the local amateur photography club.
I Good, let me just get all that down. . . drama. . . films . . . photography (pause). Now, can I assume that you'd like to work full-time with us?
A Well, I was hoping that I could work in the afternoons, if possible.
I Oh, I see. The advertisement didn't make it clear but we really need people for the mornings *and* afternoons. A lot of the flights come in quite early in the day, you see.
A Well, I suppose I *could* manage most mornings – but not Fridays, I'm afraid. I help out at an old people's home then.
I Couldn't you drop that? You'd be well-paid working for us.
A I'm afraid I couldn't really. It's not a question of money, it's voluntary work anyway, but you see they've come to rely on me and I know they'd find it difficult to get a replacement.
I I see, well I've made a note of that. . . now have you any questions you'd like to ask?
A Yes, well. . . I wonder if you could tell me what the salary would be?
I Of course, yes, I'm sorry. We'd be offering a starting salary of £115.00 a week – that's for 30 hours.
A And when you say a starting salary, do you mean that it might be increased at a later stage?
I Yes, we normally give our ground staff a month's trial and then, if everything is satisfactory we raise the salary by about 20 per cent. Any more questions?
A No – I think that's all.
I Well, thank you very much for coming in. I have got quite a lot more people to see, of course, but you should be hearing from us in about ten days. Goodbye, Miss Jones.
A Goodbye, Mr Sanderson, and thank you.

▶Unit 3 Focus on listening 1 (p. 46)

Presenter: Good evening! Welcome again to this, the last programme in our present series of 'Holiday Scene'. But we're going out in grand style. We're taking you to the fascinating island of Malta. We're taking you on a first class trip on a luxury train to Venice, and, for the more adventurous of you, we're travelling overland to India. Finally, if you're not planning to venture too far this year, we're looking at holiday deals with a difference in Scotland and Ireland.

Now, if you're one of those people with an aversion to flying, or if you suffered those frustrating delays at airports following the air traffic controllers' strike last year, why not stay on the ground this year and go by coach or train? That's what hundreds of thousands of holidaymakers do each year. In fact more people take package holidays by coach and train than go by air. For many of them the journey itself *is* the holiday. Our reporter Nick Hutchins, travelled on a very special train to Venice and he reports now from London's Victoria Station. . . FADE OUT
Reporter. . . FADE IN. . . and the scenery in this part of Scotland is really magnificent. This could be the ideal spot for those of you who want to get away from it all for a relaxing long weekend.
Presenter: Thank you, John for that report from Fort William in Scotland. And that completes our survey of holidays that have caught our attention for this programme. But let's get down to the costs.

First, that luxury train to Venice – the basic single fare, Victoria to Venice is £290. If you add to that the price of dinner and buffet lunch, you're talking about £360 per person. Even that

doesn't include the cost of wine or soft drinks with your meals, snacks or gratuities. Not cheap, but prices are relative and this must surely be a journey in a class of its own.

Next, the sunny island of Malta. A fortnight in hotel in Valetta, together with your return flight from Heathrow will cost around £192 per person. As an added bonus, car hire for a week is included at no extra charge although you'll have to pay for insurance cover.

Now for those intrepid travellers among you with the time and stamina to contemplate an overland journey to India: Chris Coles went in a party of eight in two Landrovers and the trip cost £1250 which included the hire of the camping equipment you'll need but not medical insurance so you should allow for that as an extra. You travel back by scheduled flight, by the way.

On to the Irish holiday, and the inclusive price of £142 per person here covers the cost of the ferry for your car and two passengers both to and from Ireland together with accommodation in a farmhouse of your choice. The brochure Carol mentioned gives full details of the farms and their facilities but you are advised to book early.

Finally, our visit to the West of Scotland. The cost for a 3-day stay in that splendid 17th Century castle near Fort William plus return rail fare from London is £118. The scenery, of course, comes free. Oh, and I nearly forgot to mention, children under three years old are free on both the Scottish and Irish holidays.

With that we come to the end of this programme and this series. On behalf of us all, I hope you have a very good holiday wherever you go, whatever you do. Goodbye.

▶Unit 3 Focus on listening 2 (p. 51)

A = Holiday Agent   c = Client

C I wonder if you could give me some more information about the caravan park holidays which you advertise, please.
A Yes, of course, Madam. What exactly did you want to know?
C Well, first of all, how many people can the caravans sleep? Do they vary in size?
A There are two slightly different sizes, depending on which park you choose to go to but both can accommodate up to eight people and they're both fully fitted with. . .
C (interrupting) Goodness, that's a lot! There are only four of us in our family but, all the same, I shouldn't like it to be too much of a squash. Do the beds fold up out of the way when they're not in use, to make more space?
A Some of them do but actually, in our caravans there are two entirely separate bedroom sections, so you don't need to fold the bed away, you just close the door! But I think I've got a diagram showing the layout of a typical caravan here somewhere. . . Yes, here it is. (sound of paper rustling) If you'd just like to have a look, I'll show you how it's arranged.
C Oh dear, it looks a bit complicated. Where's the door, to begin with?
A It's at the bottom of the diagram on the right, can you see? The caravan really divides up into several main areas. On the left is the lounge, that's it there. In the middle at the front is the kitchen and at the back, the bathroom. Then on the right are the two bedrooms.
C I think I see what you mean.
A Well, in the top right-hand corner there's the double bed, and next to it an L-shaped vanity unit with a mirror and drawers. On the right, just before you go out of the bedroom door, there's a small wardrobe.
C Oh is that it, marked 4?
A Yes, that's right. They key at the bottom explains the numbers.
C That seems quite roomy. . .
A Oh yes, all the fixtures and fittings have been very carefully planned to make the best use of the space available.

C And is that the second bedroom next to it, did you say?

A Yes, next to it at the shorter end. Actually that room sleeps two in bunk beds – children love them. And then, next to the bunks is another wardrobe.

C Good, there's a lot more storage space than I'd imagined. Where did you say the kitchen was?

A That's in the middle and the units are on the left of the door as you enter. There's a sink and draining board furthest from the door and the cooker is just to the left of the door. Can you see it? Between them is a cupboard.

C Well, that seems adequate. I wouldn't want to do much cooking anyway. But where can you sit down to eat? Are those three seats at the left-hand end?

A Yes, they are and the two along the longer walls of the caravan can serve as extra beds as well. No, the dining area is between the lounge and the kitchen. Perhaps I forgot to mention it. There's a table and two bench seats on either side. They're all exactly the same length on the diagram. Can you see them?

C Yes, that seems quite convenient. But what's the smaller unit separating the dining seat from the kitchen area?

A Oh, that's a cupboard – quite a large one as you can see. Handy for suitcases and so on. Well, that just leaves the bathroom to talk about. . .

C Wait a minute, what about heating? I know it's summer but you can never trust our weather, can you?

A Very true, Madam! Don't worry, there's a gas fire opposite the dining area I just showed you. It's the smallest of the three units – the other two are more cupboards.

C Fine, now what about the bathroom? Caravans often have such poor facilities.

A Not ours, Madam! Apart from a fully plumbed-in toilet, there on the right, there's a proper wash hand basin and a luxury shower unit – that's it on the left.

C Well, that all sounds very impressive. What else have I got to ask you? Oh yes, is the price of electricity and gas included in the price?

A Yes, it is but we do ask for a deposit of £25 against breakages. That's fully refundable, of course.

C Well, thank you very much for all your help. I'll have to go and discuss the whole idea with my family. Goodbye.

A Goodbye.

▶Unit 4 Focus on listening (p. 67)

P = Presenter W = Mrs White M = May

P This is the third in our series about social life in big cities and today we've come to the eastern edge of Brixton, in South London – an area of battered Victorian terraces and 1950s council flats. And here, on a particularly dreary wet Sunday afternoon, the one place positively buzzing with activity is the local coin-operated launderette.

At first sight, the laundrette seems hardly an ideal place to linger in. The walls are covered with yards of faded plastic panelling and the neon strip lights overhead cast a glare over everything. The washers are lined up in rows with foot-high benches in front so that customers sit with their backs against vibrating machines, avoiding protruding handles and the occasional leak. Icy blasts from the door cut right through to the drying area where the temperatures are easily tropical.

I spoke to one 'regular', Mrs White, and asked her what brought her to the launderette.

W D'you know, I wouldn't buy a washing machine even if I could afford one. It's not that I don't need one, goodness knows – my husband's an invalid and bed-bound and my son's a diabetic so he has spells in bed, too. No, it's just that when things get on top of me it's a great comfort to be able to get out of the house for a while and come down here to have a chat with May and Burnie.

P May and Burnie are the two lady attendants at the launderette. They each work five shifts of four hours a week. The job is really one of supervisor, reporting breakdowns to the owners, cleaning up and giving change for the machines, keeping the washing powder dispenser full and watching out for the 12-year olds who struggle in with the family wash in case they flood the place. It's very much a family business with May and Burnie as the matriarchs. They oversee their customers' activities with the practical air of ward sisters in a hospital and issue directives in soft voices; telling them the best way to fold sheets and reprimanding them when they put too much powder in the machines.

Their customers respond by obeying every word and pouring out their troubles like children. The strapping men who hand over their bags for a service wash linger for some of the advice their mother would have given:

M Those socks need darning, dear, if they're to last the winter – and next time, scrub those collars before you bring them in. They'll wash much better.

P May is knocking off and Burnie's shift is beginning. While tea is brewing an emergency conference is held:

M You know old Mrs Willis? She was in today and apparently some kids tried to kick her door down last night. She thinks they were after her pension. Frightened to death, she was. Well, I think I'll call in at the social services on my way home and see if they can help find her a flat with a caretaker and maybe a telephone entry system.

Oh, before I go, you won't forget to pop next door with some bread for Mr Soames, will you? His stomach trouble's no better.

P Burnie says she knows what she would do with young thugs. A customer joins in and they let rip together. 'Something should be done' is Burnie's favourite announcement. There's the woman who feeds best steak to her Alsatian dog and chips to her children and the man who steals his children's dinner money to buy cigarettes.

Now it seems, the launderette is under threat. It's part of a block which is to be demolished if the council has its way. I asked Burnie for her reaction. . . FADE

▶Unit 5 Focus on listening (p. 86)

Hello again, everyone! It's nice to see so many of you here on such a wet night. Well, this is the fourth week of our keep-fit class and I hope you're all beginning to feel some benefit from the exercises you've been doing. Tonight we're ready to move on to a slightly more demanding programme.

The first two exercises will provide a warm-up, as usual, and they're mainly designed to improve the flexibility and mobility in those areas of your body which are usually neglected.

Are you ready to begin?

Right! For the first exercise I'd like you to stand upright with your feet apart and your arms over your head. You'll need to leave a good distance between you. Now, bend forward to touch the floor between your feet. That's right. Right down! Bob up and down you go again to touch the floor a second time. That's it. OK you can return to your starting position again. Now, I want you to repeat that exercise nine more times. Keeping a steady rhythm. Ready? Go!

For the second exercise, stand erect with your feet apart again and your arms at your sides. Now – I want you to make large circles, with both arms at the same time, backwards and round. Come on! Really stretch those arms! Back to the starting position. Good! Now, nine more backwards circles and then nine in the opposite direction.

Now for exercise 3, I want you all lying face down. This is an exercise which will strengthen the long muscles in your back and the backs of your thighs. Stretch your arms along your sides and press your palms against your thighs. That's it. Now are you ready? Raise your head, shoulders and legs as high as possible from the floor. Keep those legs straight! Good, return *gently* to your starting position. *Gently*, I said – don't collapse! Now I want to see that movement performed eleven more times. Go!

Right, turn over on your side now for the next exercise, with your legs straight and your lower arm stretched over your head along the floor. You can use your top arm to balance yourself. That's it. Now, raise your upper leg until it's perpendicular to the floor or as near as you can manage. Come on! You can do better than that! Lower it again gently and return to your starting position. This is an exercise which concentrates on the muscles on the sides of the thighs. They're muscles that get very little work in everyday activities or in most sports, for that matter. Now, can I see that again fourteen times with the left leg. Then roll over and repeat it fourteen times with the right leg.

Next, for exercise 5, lie face down once more with your legs straight and together. This exercise is good for your arms, shoulders and chest and it also exercises your back and abdomen. I want you to get your hands directly under your shoulders. Good. Now – push your body off the floor until your arms are straightened. No – don't try to lift up your whole body. I want your hands and knees in contact with the floor. That's right. But you *must* keep your body in a straight line. Come on! This is really doing you good. Can't you feel it? OK now back to your starting position. Relax. Now, eight more push-ups please. And keep it nice and rhythmic.

Now, in this last exercise we're going to increase the flexibility in your waist area and strengthen those muscles in your hips and sides. Lie on your back with your legs straight and together and your arms stretched right out at shoulder level. Right – can you raise both legs from the floor and bend at the hips and knees. That's it. I want you to tuck them in. Now – lower your legs to the left, keeping your knees together and both shoulders on the floor. You're twisting your body over there. You *must* have your shoulders flat. That's better. Good – now raise them until they're perpendicular to the floor again and go back to your starting position. Now, can you do that seven more times? Keep your knees tucked in close to your abdomen throughout.

Good, you can all relax now for a few minutes and then we'll continue with our movement to music session. FADE

▶ Unit 6 Focus on listening (p. 105)

P = Presenter R = Reporter

P Hello and welcome to the programme which today features the latest devices designed to protect you and your property from attack.

Statistics show that a burglary takes place every 90 seconds night and day: nine out of ten break-ins are spontaneous and take less than ten minutes: and nine out of ten are through insecure doors and windows.

Tomorrow the first exhibition of its kind ever to be seen by the public, the National Crime Prevention Exhibition, will open at London's Barbican Centre and more than sixty companies will be displaying their household security systems.

The depressing truth is that household and personal security is now a boom business. The kind of devices which you can fit and remove yourself and which emit an ear-shattering screech are becoming increasingly popular and these will be represented at the exhibition along with the more conventional alarms and locks.

Our reporter, Nick Bell went along to a preview of the exhibition and here's his report. . . .

R Starting with burglar alarms, I've picked a new do-it-yourself system called Securi-home which offers good value at around £138. Its makers are so confident about it that they've struck a deal with a leading insurance company who offer reductions on house insurance to installers of the system. It has an impressive-looking box fitted to an outside wall and a slightly smaller control box. It is battery-run and an advantage is that any attempt to dismantle it or cut off the power supply automatically triggers the siren.

Next, for £8 less, the same makers offer an infra-red intruder alarm which is designed to sit on a shelf and look like a hi-fi speaker. It really is simple to install and works on batteries like the Securi-home. Anyone trying to get in sets off a 97 decibel siren.

There is also a new ultra-sonic burglar alarm which eliminates all maintenance and complex installation and guards an area of up to 600 square feet. It plugs into the mains but also has back-up alkaline battery power in case of electricity cuts. If its sonic waves are broken, an 85 decibel dual alarm sounds for 5 minutes and then resets. The alarm can only be stopped by keying in a special code. It's unobtrusive-looking in its flat rectangular box with a black casing and wood-effect panels and costs about £80.

Now, ideal for hotel rooms and caravans, is a portable door alarm. The one I've chosen is circular and made of black plastic with a fold away hanger. It hangs on the door knob and emits a 95 decibel screech if there's any movement on the door or knob. It sells for about £6.50 and is battery operated.

A slightly more sophisticated version from the same makers, called the Personal Attack Alarm, can be used on a door or as a hand-held personal alarm. It's shaped rather like a telephone receiver. The 110 decibel alarm goes off when the pressure pad is squeezed. You can only silence it by entering a personal code. It has a hanging wrist strap and contact plug for use as a door alarm. It's battery-operated and sells for about £8.

Finally, and in many ways the best design in personal alarms, is the Stopthief. It's cylindrical in shape like an aerosol and has the advantage of all battery operated devices of working when held at any angle. It gives 3¹⁄₂ minutes of continuous very very loud noise and can be obtained direct from the manufacturers at £3.99.

P Thank you, Nick, for that report on the latest in security devices. We've prepared a fact-sheet which lists all the devices mentioned together with prices and stockists and addresses to write to for further information. If you'd like a copy, just send a stamped addressed envelope to us at the following address. . . FADE

▶ Unit 7 Focus on listening (p. 126)

P = Presenter S = Steve

P Hello and welcome to this week's edition of 'Second Chance'. So far in the series we've been looking at ways in which you can go about getting the qualifications which you may have missed out on at school. We've talked about 'O' and 'A' Levels and some of the other professional certificates that you can study for part-time. Lots of you have written in to us about your experiences as mature students. Do, please, keep writing. There'll be a special programme at the end of the series featuring your letters.

Today we begin a two-part look at the opportunities which are available to mature students through the Open University. The Open University was founded in 1969 and it offers a range of courses, varying in length and type, to adults studying in their own home and in their own time. Like all universities, it awards degrees and we'll be looking at the range of degree courses in next week's programme. But today, we're going to concentrate on the pre-degree courses which the O.U. offers.

And to find out what doing such a course involves, I've invited an Open University student, Steve Marshfield, into the studio.

Steve – you've done one course already and you're now in the middle of your second. Is that right?

s Yes, I did an Arts foundation course first and now I'm doing the Social Sciences one.

p So you obviously enjoyed the experience enough to want to repeat it?

s Yes, I suppose it gets a bit compulsive (laughs). I got a lot out of the Arts foundation course – so I thought I'd have a go at something else.

p When did you leave school?

s 16.

p And that's because. . . that's what everybody did then, unless you were unusual in some way?

s Mm – well, I remember I was desperate to get out and earn some money. . .

p And if someone had said you ought to think about staying on?

s I'd probably have just giggled and said 'You must be joking!' (Laughter)

p And were you good at school?

s Oh – fair to middling. I did all right in English – I got a CSE Grade 1 – but that was the only thing I liked.

p And then when you left school, what did you do?

s Being an aspiring young socialist, I went and worked in the Co-op for a couple of years and then I worked in a storehouse for three years. Now I work in a tyre factory. Fascinating career!

p Did you have any kind of training, then, after leaving school?

s No.

p So really this was the first time you'd ever had to get down to study. Was that hard?

s Yes it was, it was hard and it's gonna be even harder. . .

p Yes.

s As it goes on.

p What's hard especially? Is it the discipline?

s Yes, it's the discipline of switching from being a manual labourer to a mental labourer.

p Yes.

s It's difficult to do.

p How did you hear about the Open University?

s I used to see the programmes on the television when I got in from the night shift. They're on from twenty past seven to quarter to eight on Thursdays.

p Is that the only time they're shown?

s No they're shown on Sunday mornings from five to nine to twenty past. But it's a repeat of Thursday's. Anyway, I thought I'd like to know more about this.

p And how did you choose a course? How much choice is there?

s Well there are five or six foundation courses. You have to do a foundation course before going on to a degree. There's a Social Sciences foundation course, an Arts one, Maths, Science and Technology. . . Oh and Education. I took the one I was interested in – the Arts. Literature mainly. I drew a total blank with the philosophy. I enjoyed it but it was very very tough. And it wasn't put across very well either. There was far too much assumption that we were all hyper-intelligent.

p How much time do you need to spend a week on a course?

s Well, you're supposed to do a unit a week and they say to allow 15 hours a unit. But I just haven't got that amount of time to spare – not without *completely* reorganising my life, anyway. I reckon you can get away with two-thirds – a minimum of 10 hours. A good Saturday and Sunday.

p What was your family's reaction to your doing the course?

s Well, I live at home with my parents. They don't really understand at all!

p But they're not negative. . . ?

s No, but they're not particularly positive, either I mean, they're not at all intellectual. My mum's only ever read one book in her life. Mind you, she quite enjoys some of the programmes.

p So she watches them with you?

s She has to. The telly's in the kitchen!

p And how about the people at work, in the tyre factory?

s I haven't told them.

p Why not?

s I think they'd send me up about it – start calling me 'the Professor', or something.

p How did you get on with the exam at the end of the course?

s I completely fluffed the exam. I made an absolute hash of it! I did pass the course but I realise now that it was in spite of the exam. I realise that because I had a letter from the Dean of the Arts Faculty telling me that, very nicely, that though I'd passed, I only passed absolutely minimally!

p You say you fluffed the exam. Can you pinpoint why?

s Well, I went in there in completely the wrong frame of mind. I was just completely apathetic. I *sat* there and wrote for 3 hours but it's only when you get outside you think 'Oh no, did I really say that?'

p And on the money side, how much was the course?

s I think for this year, it's £133 for a full course, £87 for summer school, £5 or £6 for books and then, you know, as much as you want to spend on pens. . .

p Do you think it's good value – for what you get?

s It makes it quite an expensive hobby! It's just a pity there aren't more grants available. I mean, I think the Open University *was* started for people like me. If I was married with a family and a mortgage there'd be no way I could do it and there's no way I'd get help, either.

p You could probably get a grant to go to an ordinary university now. If you were offered a place, would you jump at the chance?

s No, I wouldn't jump at it. I'd consider it. The thing is, for me, it'd be very difficult to go into higher education now that I've had 10, 12 years of having money in my pocket.

p Yes.

s 'Cos it'd be an enormous change in my lifestyle and probably one that'd be difficult to cope with.

p Yes. And finally, Steve, have you any advice you'd like to give to someone who was thinking of taking an O.U. course?

s (Pause) Yes. Hold your nose and jump in!

p (Laughs) Thank you very much for talking to me, Steve.

▶ Unit 8 Focus on listening (p. 143)

TL = Tour Leader G = Member of group

TL Well, I think you've seen everything there is to see here in the studio, ladies and gentlemen, but I mustn't forget to mention that the person in charge here, the person who controls the performers and the technicians, is the floor manager. He acts as the producer's representative, in effect, because the producer is not actually on the studio floor, of course. He directs the programme from the control room or gallery, as it's usually known.

And, if you'd like to follow me, we'll go up and have look at the control room now.
(Sounds of shuffling and people moving off)

Right! Are we all here now? Good. Well this is the nerve centre of the whole television operation. As you can see, the window gives the producer a bird's eye view of what's happening below on the studio floor. That's if there isn't a convenient bit of the set right in the way – which sometimes happens!

You'll notice that the lighting here is quite subdued in contrast to the glare of the studio. That's so that the producer and his – or her, I should say – technical crew can watch the TV screens or monitors in front of them.

As you can see, the control room divides into two halves, basically, separated by that curved table. On one side there's a bank of monitors in two rows; the bottom row registers the pictures taken by each camera in the studio and the numbers on the monitors show which camera the picture is coming from. In the top row, in the middle, is the transmission monitor. That's the monitor which shows the pictures which are actually being recorded – the picture the viewer sees, in other words.

On the left is a monitor which shows pre-recorded material from videotape or other sources; and on the right is a special preview monitor which shows the next shot chosen for recording. And then, behind the table, directly facing the monitors is where the production staff sit. Working from the left-hand side, as we look towards the screens, first of all we have one or two people in charge of make up, wardrobe and design – you'll remember seeing those sections, earlier. Next is the production secretary – she's the producer's personal assistant. Then, the producer himself. He speaks into the microphone in front of him so that everyone wearing earphones in the studio and in the vision and sound control rooms can hear him. In a simple programme, the producer will normally direct cameras himself. With more complicated programmes and long-running series, there are separate directors who are responsible for the work in the studio.

Finally, on the extreme right hand side is one of the technical managers who is in charge of the cameramen and all the technical details in the studio.

Are there any questions?

G Yes. What's this panel of switches and things on the table here?

TL Sorry, yes. Those are used for cutting from camera to camera, or from camera to film, to change the image on the transmission monitor. The vision mixer sits here in front of them and it's his job to operate them. He, or more often she, is a key person in the control room, in fact.

OK – now if you could all turn round, away from the monitors, and look towards the back of the room for a moment, you'll see a separate little cubicle. That's where the technical staff in charge of lighting work. They have an absolute barrage of controls and monitors around them but you'll have to take my word for it I'm afraid, because we're running rather short of time. Anyway, you remember me saying that studio lights are set at particular angles before rehearsals begin? Well, the lighting department has the job of switching them and on and off during transmission, varying their intensity and so on.

Finally, on the far side of the room, there's another cubicle for the sound supervisor. Can you see? To the side of the monitors?

The sound engineers have to chose which microphones to use and check that they produce natural sound. They also listen for the sort of noises which might spoil a production – heavy footsteps, chairs scraping – you know.

We'll be able to take a look inside as we go out but this concludes our tour of the studio and control room. I hope you've found it interesting.

Fine, well if you'd like to follow me, we'll make our way round by the sound engineers' room and downstairs where I think there's a cup of tea waiting for us. . . FADE

▶Unit 9 Focus on listening 1 (p. 165)

Salt is a substance well-known to everyone because of its characteristic taste – one of the four basic tastes which our tongues are able to detect, in fact. Sodium chloride, the familiar white substance we use in cooking, is known as 'common salt' to distinguish it from the many other chemical compounds which are also classed as 'salts'.

Salt is by no means rare, of course. It is to be found in the rock formations of all ages in almost inexhaustible quantities. Yet salt has been called 'the world's most valuable mineral' because of its importance to the health of man and his animals, as well as for his industries.

When we perspire, we exude salt and this can even form crystals on the skin of some people as the perspiration dries.

Similarly, tears contain salt. A deficiency of salt is harmful to the body yet an excess can be fatal. If we drank sea water for a few days – and sea water contains only about 3% common salt – we would certainly die.

Salt is a flavouring without which a lot of our meals would seem tasteless and it is an important preservative used in the food and leather industries. Spread on the roads in winter, it effectively thaws ice and snow and reduces the risk of accidents.

The importance of salt made it a major trading commodity all over Europe and Africa from earliest times, and it was exchanged for slaves, textiles and gold. Even nowadays, nomads in Ethiopia transport salt by camel, mule and donkey along a 125-mile trail, as they have done for a thousand years. They also use bricks of salt in a single piece or broken up into smaller sections as a hard currency whose exchange rate does not vary.

Supplies of salt occur in two main forms – rock salt, the remnants of seas that have dried up, and sea water or 'brine'. (The two greatest brine lakes of the world are the Dead Sea of Jordan and the Great Salt Lake of the USA.) In the past, most salt was usually obtained by allowing sun and wind to evaporate sea water in shallow pools or 'salterns', constructed by the side of the sea or estuaries. This system is still followed in warm countries, particularly in India, China and on the shores of the Mediterranean and the Red Sea. Evaporation of the sea leaves the salts concentrated as a solid and this is collected.

The bulk of present day world production, however, is rock salt, which can either be dug out by mining or obtained by forcing water into salt layers and recovering it as brine. Certain rock salt deposits, incidentally, are of interest to oil prospectors since they may indicate the presence of oil nearby.

The purity of rock salt is increased by refining it and, as refined salt easily absorbs moisture from the atmosphere, a small percentage of magnesium carbonate is often added to keep the salt running freely. The finished product is very different from our ancestors' salt which was brownish, stained with earth and damp.

▶Unit 9 Focus on listening 2 (p. 168)

Europe has no other salt marsh landscape that can compare in beauty, individuality and historical significance with that on the French Atlantic coast. Today only a few islands are left of the once continuous production area between the estuary of the Gironde in the south and the Gulf of Morbihan in the north. Perhaps it's the salterns of Brittany that today convey the clearest impression of the methods of operation of the original salt marshes.

In a typical Brittany saltern, sea water flows by gravity through an intricate sequence of storage, concentration and crystallisation units. Locks control the supply of water from one selection of the system to another. The highest, outermost unit is the storage pond, where the sea water is first introduced. Normal high water does not reach its inlets; only the spring tide, which is exceptionally high, can fill it. At the lowest, and innermost point of the system are the crystallisation beds where evaporation leaves the salt concentrated as a solid. It's from the bottom of these beds that the salt-worker scrapes the salt with a flat-edged rake and collects it. By the time the brine has passed from the concentration beds and reached the crystallisation beds its salt content is already eight times as great as it was in the storage pond. Accurate assessment of its degree of concentration is the first condition of successful salt-making, for any salt that crystallises out too soon, in the pools that serve only for concentration, will be mixed with sludge and slime. If instead, the saltworker leaves the brine too long in the crystallisation beds, the common salt will be followed by other, undesirable salts which will considerably reduce the value of his product.

The Breton saltworker's year begins in spring.

The ponds and beds then have to be drained – and this a very laborious job, since there are no natural outlets and all the water must be ladled out by hand. Next, the parts of the salterns consisting of shaped mud – that is, the walls and beds of the ponds and the dams between them – all this must be cleaned and weeded, smoothed, trodden and beaten into shape. The first salt yield comes only in June, *after* a preconcentration period of anything up to seven weeks, according to the hours of sunshine. If the weather is good – plenty of sun, plenty of wind – the beds will go on producing salt regularly every second or third day till late in September. Once it has been harvested, the salt is left to dry in bright heaps on the causeways between the beds and later on the edges of the concentration ponds. Sometimes it may even be kept there through the winter, protected by a covering of reeds and soil.

▶Unit 10 Focus on listening (p. 187)

w = Woman m = Man s = Mrs Stewart j = Jack

w Hello–Among our problems tonight, the disappearing salesman, who's landed a young mother with a mountain of debt, and there are hundreds of others, it now seems.

m And the story of the amazing shrinking suit.

w And the stamp club parcel that became a nightmare for our listener. He didn't have it, he didn't want it and he didn't owe for it but a debt collection agency threatened to make life very unpleasant for him unless he paid for it just the same.
But first, a complaint from a young mother at Redfield which has turned out to be the tip of an iceberg affecting hundreds of people all over Britain. The Fraud Squad are now investigating and in a moment they'll be asking for your help so have a pen ready.

m The story concerns a catalogue distributed by a firm called Tinyware Products and the activities of a Mr Albert Brown. The upshot of it is that our listener, Mrs Linda Stewart, has forked out a total of £615 and all she has to show for it is a very shoddy pushchair.

w It began when Mrs Stewart saw an advertisement in a magazine for the Tinyware range. To cut a long story short, she not only ordered a large number of items for herself, she paid out £230 to Mr Brown to become the firm's agent in the Redfield area.

m Mrs Stewart needed the money to keep herself and her young daughter but the goods she ordered didn't turn up. Not just her own, but pushchairs and other items she ordered on behalf of her customers. Not only is she now in financial trouble but she feels responsible for the money she collected. And Mr Brown can't be found.
Mrs Stewart, what happened when Mr Brown came to see you?

s Well, he came and he told me about the products. He was very enthusiastic which got me very keen too, so I decided to become an agent.

n Was it going to cost you any money?

s Yes. £230. He didn't demand it. But to get the ball rolling, I thought 'OK, give him the money, get on with it'. Because I couldn't go out to work – with having a baby – she was my responsibility – so I thought I could do it from home. It was my only chance.

m Now, before meeting Mr Brown you'd in fact ordered some goods. You'd only received one of those – it was a pushchair. What did you think of it?

s It was – alright – but it wasn't worth the money really. It was really flimsy with a real look of cheapness about it and the fittings were none too solid.

m Did many people want to buy these pushchairs?

s Yes, there were 5 orders for pushchairs alone.

m Was there any sign of the goods?

s The one pushchair. That was all. He kept promising me and assuring me and reassuring me that there'd been a few delays but now everything was set to take off. And – emm – like a fool, I believed him.

m At what stage did you become suspicious?

s Em – when I received a letter from the Post Office saying that – em – my registered letter had been sent back and the Fraud Squad were involved. And then the next day I received a 5-page statement to fill in from the Fraud Squad.

m What did they say about Mr Brown?

s Just that he was a con-man. They'd discovered that his so-called business premises was an ordinary flat with nothing in it and no-one there.

m Did they mention that other people had fallen foul?

s Yes, well they said 400 but I could believe there's more. Looking back on it, it makes me feel very bitter. Not because I've been conned, but because he knew my circumstances.

w Despite all our efforts, we've been unable to find the elusive Mr Brown. The magazine which published the advertisement say they've had dozens of complaints and they'll compensate anyone who can prove they've lost money so that's some small comfort to Mrs S., who'll at least get back the money for the goods which she ordered for herself.

m But the Fraud Squad are now asking for *your* help. They've already had hundreds of complaints from all over Britain. If you've lost money or know anything about Mr Albert Brown or Tinyware Products, they'd like to hear from you.

w Next in the postbag this week comes a plea from Mrs Bowen who claims that she's been taken to the cleaners, literally!

m And it's all over a suit which Mrs Bowen bought for her 18 year old son, a student. The first time it came back from the dry cleaners, she says. . .

w It'd shrunk at least 3 inches. My son just can't wear it at all now. It cost £90 and I can't afford to go and buy another one.

m And since then, Mrs Bowen has gone back and forth without success.

w I took it back to the tailor's. They sent it away for testing. They now claim it's the cleaner's fault. I went back to the cleaner's and they say it's the manufacturer's.

m Mrs Bowen says the suit is now useless to her son. Everyone says it's someone else's fault. Please can you advise me? Jack, what's your advice?

j Well this poor lady has now become the ping pong ball between the manufacturer and the cleaners, hasn't she? And that is quite unsatisfactory. The manufacturers, to be fair, took the suit back and they tested it and they've now made their assertion. Inside the suit, quite properly, there is a label which tells you precisely what the suit is made of and how to dry clean it. And I think the dry cleaners have behaved in a fairly peremptory manner in this matter. They've just said 'Oh it's not our fault.' And this poor lady is left holding the suit which is now looking rather a mess, quite honestly. What ought to happen is that the two concerns should get together to establish if the label is correct. And if it is correct, was it cleaned correctly? These are not things she can establish. It's not fair that she should be treated like this.

w Thank you Jack. Next what we think is an extraordinary example of the methods some firms use to recover debts. Threats which almost amount to blackmail. Enough to alarm most people. And all the more inexcusable when it turns out to be demands for money which our listener never owed in the first place. Just listen to this for a sentence:

M Unless we receive full payment for the full amount within seven days of your receiving this letter, we will issue a summons against you without further notice. Service will take place at your home or place of employment.

w At your place of employment – imagine the embarrassment it would cause! Well that threat came from a firm called Access Debt Services Ltd. And it all began when a package dropped through the letter box of Mr Walters of Southleigh. It was from the Collector's Forum Stamp Club. Very odd because as Mr Walters says:

M I'd resigned from the club many months before. I didn't open the package. I sent it straight back.

w And that was the last he heard until the letter arrived, threatening court action unless he paid £9.85. It says:

M 'An adverse court judgement would then make it extremely difficult for you to obtain credit from other sources.'

w We spoke to the Collectors' Forum Stamp Club and they said:

M He does owe us money.

w Have you checked?

M Mistakes do occur. We get 1500 books a month being returned.

w Which speaks volumes, if you'll pardon the pun, about the difficulties which can occur when people try and cancel their membership of some book and stamp clubs. Anyway, to cut a long story short, Collectors' Forum now accept that Mr Walters doesn't owe them any money and he's now been showered with apologies.

J Well, I'll bet he has and for very good reason, you see, because they're now in a difficulty, really. It seems to me they may well have committed two offences. First of all demanding payment for unsolicited goods and secondly sending a threatening letter. I've seen some debt letters in my time and I think this is one of the most disgraceful I've ever seen quite honestly. This is harassment of the consumer. What is he saying? I'll serve a summons in front of your workmates. That'll humiliate you, won't it? Furthermore I'll make sure you never buy anything else on credit. This is absolutely dreadful. This is the sort of situation which calls for an investigation because this company gets 1500 packages back a month. Are all these 1500 people getting this sort of letter? I sincerely hope not!

w Well, that's it for this week. Remember, our lines are open until 9.30 this evening if you have anything you'd like our advice about. And now, from all of us, goodbye.

Exam Practice Tapescripts

►Home improvements (p. 201)

CG = Cynthia Greenway GN = George Neal

Part 1

CG Hello and welcome to 'Home Front'. I'm Cynthia Greenway and in our programme today, we'll be looking at the subject of home improvements.

Open almost any newspapers these days and you'll find advertisements inviting you to install a new kitchen, to have your loft converted into an extra room or even to invest in a swimming pool. But will these 'extras' actually add to the value of your house when you come to sell it? Here in the studio is George Neal of the estate agent's Brandon and White to provide some expert advice.

George, first of all, how *do* you go about deciding the price of a house?

GN Well Cynthia, house pricing isn't an exact science by any means. We can look at the sort of house it is, its size and condition, of course, but where it is is also very important and a great deal depends on the state of the market. And then fashion comes into it too. . . .

CG Yes, can you give us some examples of changes in fashion?

GN Well, as far as kitchen units and kitchen furniture are concerned, formica and plastic, however expensive they are, are out. Natural wood is still in, for the time being, at least, and a traditional cast-iron kitchen stove is *very* fashionable. In the bathroom, coloured bathroom suites – especially all those mud coloured ones – are definitely out. Old-fashioned baths, you know the ones with elegant legs, are very much back in fashion. And as for decoration, patterned wallpaper and patterned tiles are out. Plain white or plain pastel shades are now the thing.

CG I see.

Part 2

CG And what are the items which actually add to the value of a house?

GN Ah, that's where people often make a mistake. They can spend a fortune on luxury extras, expecting to increase the value of their property, and when they come to sell it, they may find that it makes no difference to the price. Worse still, they may even find that the expensive addition actually makes it harder to sell their property!

CG OK. Tell us about the improvements it's worth making then, George, if you will. What about the little touches of luxury in the bathroom for instance? I must admit I've always fancied having gold taps – you know, the ones with swans' heads and things on them, but. . .

GN . . . cost a fortune!

CG . . . True. But would it be worthwhile? I mean, would it make people want to buy my house more?

GN No, sorry Cynthia, but I doubt if it would have any effect at all. If you *want* that sort of thing in your bathroom, then you must do it for your own satisfaction. And the same can be said for other extravagant extras like a turbo-charged sink, or a black sunken Jacuzzi or a patio, – even a swimming pool (remember they take a lot of maintenance!). Personalise your house for your own pleasure by all means, but don't expect to recoup the money you've spent when you sell the house.

CG That surprises me, I must say. But it's a useful warning. Now let's imagine I live in a fairly typical house – 3 bedrooms, say, in a suburban area. What improvements would you recommend?

GN Well, it's worth considering having a conservatory built on, especially if there's no proper dining room. That's a very attractive feature. And if you've got a loft, or space in the roof, then I should definitely think of having a roof conversion. You'd gain an extra room and, as with the conservatory, you'd certainly get your money back at the very least, when you came to sell.

CG What about knocking down the wall between the kitchen and dining room, so that you've got one big room – that seems to be popular these days?

GN Yes, that's quite a good idea, especially if you've got young children and want to keep an eye on them while you're cooking. It makes it more of a family room. That can increase the value.

CG And putting in a downstairs loo?

GN Unlikely to add any extra but at the same time an extra downstairs toilet is quite a good selling point so it may well help to make a quick sale.

CG How about fitted cupboards?

GN Yes, people are always very concerned about the amount of cupboard space in a house, and fitted cupboards are a definite plus. People expect them these days, in fact.

CG Incidentally, is there any advantage in including your carpets when you sell your house?

GN Actually, people are tending more and more to look for houses with everything thrown in. Curtains and carpets are so expensive these days. Again, like the fitted cupboards, including these things probably won't add to the value but there's a good chance it will help you to sell more quickly.

CG And we haven't talked about the garden. Are gardens important?

GN Oh yes, the garden can be a very important factor. But it's easy to go over the top with gardens, like everything else. If you pay to have it designed to cut down on maintenance, you'll probably get your money back. But if you start going in for little goldfish ponds or ornamental fountains, then I wouldn't rely on it! There's another thing to say about gardens, too. A lot of people plant trees a foot or so away from the house, quite forgetting that they grow to oh, 30 feet. These quick growing jobs can actually detract from the price, because they can make a house look depressing and dark.

CG And still on gardens, or at least plants: it always looks appealing when you read 'wisteria covered' in the estate agent's brochure. Is it worth planting wisteria or some other kind of climbing plant so that it grows over the front of your house?

GN Well, it sounds fine, certainly, and looks nice too. But if the surveyor points out that the wisteria is pulling away the mortar from the walls, then the buyer may not be so keen. He may reduce his offer, in fact.

Part 3

CG OK, Now what about the older type of property – a cottage in the country, for example?

GN Well, obviously the first thing to do with an older property is to deal with any structural defects because otherwise it won't get past the purchaser's surveyor. And after that, it's important to remember that presentation is everything. It's those first 5 minutes that count, and if a buyer has taken against the house in those crucial moments, no amount of pointing out the hand-carved kitchen units will help. It *will* help, though, if the place has been mistreated, for example, to take out those awful modern metal windows and other horrors and replace them with traditional looking ones.

It's also worth making a cottage bigger if possible, by clever use of space – making 3 bedrooms out of 2 for example – though not if you end up with two tiny poky rooms instead of 1 decent-sized one! It's worth aiming for a clean crisp look throughout with plenty of white paint. You can add

35 – 50% to the price of a cottage doing it up, but an awful lot can be done cosmetically.

CG Thank you, George, for that invaluable advice. And you can send for our factsheet on home improvements – we'll give you the address later. But now we move on to the fascinating subject of drains. . . .

▶ Time is money (p. 202)

SO = Interviewer AB = Adrian Burchall

SO Right, Adrain, you are a horologist, is that correct?

AB Yes, it is.

SO Yes, how what's the – an easier way of saying that?

AB A clockmaker, I suppose.

SO A clockmaker, and does, does that mean you actually make clocks?

AB No, not really. Ah, most people who call themselves clockmakers today do not actually make them, but are engaged in the business of repairing...

SO Mhm.

AB And selling them and this has been the situation for a very long time.

SO I see. What are the main kinds of clocks that you deal with?

AB Mostly English Grandfather and Longcase clocks and, but also other types of English...

SO Mhm.

AB And French, particularly, clocks.

SO Mhm, what's a Longcase clock?

AB A Longcase clock is a weightdriven either eight day duration or thirty hour duration – clock which and. . . .

SO So it's...

AB And the casing really is a means of enclosing the weights and the pendulum and the movement itself.

SO Yes and are there clocks that you do deal with but not in the same quantities?

AB Oh yes, that's probably right.

SO What, what would they be?

AB Mostly either English Bracket or Mantle clocks. . . .

SO Mhm.

AB As they are more generally called by non horologists, and wall clocks also.

SO Mhm.

AB And French carriage clocks and Mantle clocks and – I will look at any clock that anybody wishes to bring in to me and. . .

SO Do you even deal with modern ones?

AB Tell them what I think about it, – not so much no. . . .

SO Mhm, mhm.

AB Not so much not many clocks made after the last war.

SO And do, do you find yourself horrified at the state of some clocks when you are asked to look at them?

AB I'm afraid I do but it's what I'm in business for and, I try to help my customers whenever possible.

SO What's the, the worst example of neglect you've seen for a clock?

AB There have been so many of those it would be impossible to single out any particular example, I think. But it's really quite easy, given unfavourable storage conditions for, for clock cases particularly to fall into a very bad state of repair in quite a short period of time. They can be quite perishable when, when you have damp and, this is undoubtedly how some of them get in a very bad state and once the damp sets in you have pieces start to drop, drop off and then they get lost and sadly they can be quite difficult to put right in those situations, that sort of situation.

SO And have you any funny, funny stories about, clocks that you've found?

AB Well, one or two. It's amazing how, or perhaps not all that extraordinary how people regard their clocks as people, and having, having a will of their own almost. But, I remember once I used to look after, and still do, a clock in a chapel in Bristol and I went in one day and I found a new verger in there and he said to me 'Oh the erm, the clock has stopped, could you please have a look at it?' So I said, 'certainly'. He said, 'Now the most extraordinary thing happened,' he said, 'I was taking over from my predecessor and on his last day at work he was going to show me the ropes, so I came in a day early and the following day when I came in, the clock had stopped and the terrible thing was that, my predecessor, the previous verger, had in fact died during the night'. . . .

SO Ah.

AB 'On his – after his last day at work. So since then,' he said, 'I know that's several weeks ago, I haven't touched the clock or done anything to it at all,' he said, 'I don't know what it is, but I, I just felt that there was – I couldn't do anything.' So I looked at the clock and I thought, well I wonder if it's wound-up, so I wound it and I wound it and I wound it and I wound it all the way up to the top and, lo and behold that was the trouble and obviously, the verger having died had not been able to wind the clock up so the clock had stopped.

SO That's a lovely story. And do people ever do foolish things with their clocks?. . . Do they keep things inside the cases or...?

AB Yes, curiously enough, it's, it's a place that, that thieves, who break into a house, always look inside a grandfather clock you know.

SO Is it?

AB Because they imagine that people keep things down in the bottom, keep money. You can invariably, if a grandfather clock is, standing in a house which has been burgled, you quite, the police quite often know the time that it took place because the thieves will have opened the door. And they will have interfered with the pendulum, not intentionally, but while they're rummaging around in the bottom to see if there is anything there and then the clock will stop at that precise time.

SO So it's not recommended to keep things in clocks?

AB No, it's a sure place they will look certainly.

SO And I just wanted to ask you one last question and that is would you recommend, your career to other young people?

AB Well it's certainly a very interesting career to anybody who is interested in the field, but it is very time consuming and is, is not a very lucrative one, even though the repairs are costly, the time involved in doing them is, so great that, a lot, a lot of people would not consider it to be very worth while.

SO So it has to be, for the love of it really.

AB Well to use that particular expression, yes.

SO Thank you.

▶Himalayan kingdoms (p.203)

SB = Tour leader SO = Client

Part 1

SB Come in.

SO Is this Himalayan Kingdoms?

SB Hello yes, yes, come on in.

SO Gosh, it's a long way up.

SB Yeah, it certainly is, isn't it.

SO I've got, some questions really. I had your brochure and I'd like to ask you a few questions about it, is that all right?

SB Yes, please, take a seat.

SO Thanks. Well, the brochure's really exciting, I mean I find it very hard to believe that, that, you can go to the Himalayas for an ordinary holiday and that you don't need to be super-fit, which the brochure says, is that right?

SB Yes, that, that's, yeah that's quite right.

SO So, what kind of people usually go on holidays like this?

SB All sorts of people, actually. I think the, the general thing is that people tend to be over the age of thirty.

SO Mhm.

SB And can be up to, you know, over the age of sixty

SO So what would be your minimum age range?

SB Minimum fifteen. We don't, we don't really want to take children.

SO Yes. And – how do you know if people are fit enough, do you just have to rely on, on their say–so or do you require medical certificates?

SB We only require a medical certificate if they're over the age of sixty.

SO Mhm.

SB And apart from that, I mean the treks are graded so that, they can get some idea of how fit they need to be.

SO Yes, I was going to ask you about that actually, – you've got four grades, haven't you?

SB Yeah.

SO I wonder if you can just, just say bit more because I wasn't quite sure whether – what the difference was I suppose, between easy and reasonable and vigorous.

SB Yes, well, it's basically the number of hours you'd do per day.

SO Mhm.

SB The number of consecutive days trekking. . .

SO Yes.

SB And the sort of heights that, that a trek will go to, the number of high passes, and, and and so on, whether you have to go on snow or not. So the easy treks are basically, probably only five or six days' consecutive trekking. . .

SO Yes.

SB On easy terrain, that, fairly level terrain, only very small passes. . . probably not above, ten or eleven thousand feet.

SO So you – would you need to acclimatize for the easy type of trekking?

SB Well most, most people find ten or eleven thousand feet quite happy to deal with. . .

SO Mhm.

SB Not many people have difficulty with that. It's once you get up to sort of fourteen, fifteen thousand that people start to feel the effects of altitude, the average human being. I mean there are people that suffer at eleven or twelve, there are people who can go up to twenty six with absolutely no trouble.

SO And what happens then if somebody does suffer from the altitude, do they just have to wait till they get over it, or...

SB Well, the trips are all designed to go slowly up to altitude anyway, to, to give people acclimatization, but there are, there, there will be one individual in a thousand or one individual in every five hundred who, who, who doesn't acclimatize, and they would have to be taken back down again.

SO Yes that must be pretty disappointing.

SB But it's a pretty rare thing, actually I mean most people suffer from headaches, I mean I suffer from the occasional headache.

SO Mhm.

Part 2

SO So, well, let me think about this, I, I have to tell you that I'm really interested in the Himalayan summit tour which is classed as strenuous, and I don't know really whether, that's realistic or practical.

SB Well, looking at you, I mean I should imagine that you'd be able do to it.

SO So it doesn't need – you don't need to be super fit?

SB You don't need to be super fit, you need to have, a love of walking, you know, and able to walk long distances.

SO OK, well, there's a, a map in the, in the brochure, which in fact shows various routes, I wasn't quite sure. . . with this – Himalayan summit one you – you fly to Srinagar?

SB Srinagar, yes.

SO That's, yes, and what happens after that?

SB After that, after a bit of a rest at Srinagar you, you take a road journey. . . .

SO Yes.

SB Over the Zoji La Pass which is thirteen and a half thousand. . .

SO Oh yes.

SB And, and on through the sort of mountains there through to a place called Kargil.

SO Oh I can see it, yes.

SB Then you stop overnight there.

SO Where – how would you travel, actually?

SB Well, it'll be private transport, it'll probably be jeeps or, or perhaps a truck.

SO Mhm hm. And where would you stay in Kargil?

SB The Caravanserai Hotel!

SO Yes, right, and from there?

SB And then from there, carry on by road, over a number of high passes, the Fotu La Pass, which is about fourteen and a half thousand, following the Indus river and, and through the mountains, through to the capital of Ladakh which is a place called Leh.

SO Yes, I can see, yes. That's got an airport as well.

SB And that's got a small airport, yes, and then we stay in a hotel there – sorry, no, what am I saying, what am I saying. . . from Kargil we go through to a place called Lamayuru. . . .

SO Ah yes, it's not far.

SB Where there's a large monastery, OK, and then we, we get out there and we do a trek that is four or five days long through the villages and over a number of high passes.

SO Is that Wanla and Alchi?

SB Wanla and Alchi, that's, that's right. So that's basically to get people a bit fit, acclimitized, they'll go up to an altitude of almost fifteen thousand feet, and then they'll join the road again at Alchi where they'll be picked up by private transport, taken on to Leh...

SO Yes.

SB And, have a rest in Leh for a day and then, from there we go by jeep across the Indus valley to a place called Stok. . .

SO Yes.

SB Where the old palace is, the king's old palace still owned by the, the present queen in fact, it's a museum now, and then two days' walking up the, the valley, a sort of a series of narrow. . .

SO Mhm.

SB Defiles and and valleys that take you up towards a mount – this mountain called Stok Kangri which is the. . .

SO Oh yes.

SB Highest mountain in that range of mountains just south of Leh.

SO Mhm mhm.

SB But there's a very easy or very straightforward way up the back of the mountain – it looks quite impressive from Leh but actually it's very straightforward on the back.

SO Yes.

SB It's just a, you know, simple walking. . .

SO And how long does that take?

SB Up snow. We spend a day in camp, acclimatizing, at base camp, seventeen and a half thousand feet, and then up to the summit is about seven hours.

SO Right. And you stay the night where?

SB And then you descend again back down to base camp.

SO All in one day?

SB All in one day, yes, I mean the descent takes about three hours. . .

SO Yes.

SB And then. . .

SO Then you. . .

SB Then back down to Stok, back to Leh, fly over the Himalayas, back to Srinagar.

SO Oh, it sounds wonderful!

SB Yeah, you should do it.

Part 3

SO Well, let me just ask you a little bit more. The, the price covers all the flights?

SB Yes.

SO And all the transport and all the accommodation, does it?

SB Yes, that's right.

SO And the equipment?

SB And the equipment and all the food.

SO And all the food.

SB All bar the main meals in Delhi, the evening meals in Delhi.

SO Right. And is there anything else that isn't covered that I ought to add on?

SB Airport tax, Indian airport tax, which is about five quid, which for practical purposes is better paid by yourself than by us.

SO Insurance, I suppose.

SB Insurance, which is about, I think for that trip is forty one pounds fifty.

SO Mhm. Cheap at the price!

SB Yes.

SO And, what about, visas?

SB Yes, and visa, you need to get an Indian visa, which is, twenty pounds.

SO All right, and what about spending money, how much should allow for that?

SB Well there's not a lot to spend your money on, actually, in Ladakh, I mean the only things that you'd be spending it on would be beer and post cards, so I don't know, five pounds a day, perhaps.

SO Right.

SB I mean you'd you'd have bags to spare.

SO Good, OK. And if I'm interested in doing this, when's the next one?

SB You mean the next tour?

SO Yes.

SB The Himalayan Summit Tour?

SO Mhm.

SB Can I just check that, I'm not sure of the dates, ah, the dates, ah, Saturday the sixth of August. . .

SO Right.

SB To Saturday the twenty seventh of August.

SO OK, and when do I need to book up by?

SB Well, two months in advance is the, is the deadline, really.

SO Right.

SB Any time between now and then.

SO Fine. Good. Thank you very much.

SB OK. Pleasure.

▶ A Many-Sided Therapy (p. 205)

MM = Osteopath I = Interviewer M = Mark (patient)

Part 1

MM Well, basically, the body has its own mechanism of righting itself, and people who go to see their doctors or their osteopaths or whoever, have somehow lost their way in righting themselves. For instance, if you cut yourself, your body will heal itself by forming a clot. Or, if you have cirrhosis of the liver and they cut away part of the your liver, it will grow again. So basically there is some kind of barrier that is preventing your body from healing itself. A doctor will give you a chemical remedy to alleviate the pain or to act as a catalyst, and an osteopath will simply attempt to remove the barriers to health.

I   Well, you've given us two examples there, where they are organs of the body that are affected. Are you concerned about the body as a whole? Would someone come to an osteopath if they had something wrong, well say with their liver?

MM   Yes, they might well do and it's important to realise that the symptoms somebody is presenting with are symptoms of a liver disfunction. It's important to treat the body as a whole. For instance, somebody might have a nutritional problem that you'd need to deal with looking closely at their diet, or more than just a physical problem, they may have some kind of psychological problem as well that you will need to coax them along with and help them recover from.

I   But to go back to this idea that there is a barrier, there is a breakdown in the body being able to heal itself, will someone always come to an osteopath in pain?

MM   No, not at all. Quite often people come to the osteopath last of all. Often we're the end of the line. People have gone through the normal system of seeing their doctor, perhaps having some physiotherapy, having X-rays, seeing a physiotherapist, and perhaps due to the fact that you have to wait a long time to have treatment on the health service, sometimes people will come along to an osteopath and they don't necessarily need to be in a lot of pain – their problems may be well-hidden.

I   And what are you going to do once they get here?

MM   Well, what I'll do is first of all I'll take a detailed case history to give myself some idea of the problem, and once I've assured myself that there's nothing more seriously wrong with the person than a back problem, or a problem related to their back, I will examine their back and see if I can find the barriers to health.

I   Well it's interesting that we've gone through a basic introduction to osteopathy and you've only just now mentioned the back, when most people will immediately think it's, if you've got back pain see your osteopath. Why didn't you simply say 'People come to me with back pains'?

MM   Well no it's not, the back is just one part of your body and osteopathy, like many of the other complementary therapies, are holistic therapies and people can have all sorts of problems related to their backs such as lung conditions, heart conditions or even peripheral problems like ankle pains and just simple joint pains. The back is just one aspect – it's a very multi-faceted therapy.

I   Well in fact we have got someone who has got something wrong with their back. Mark has come along with me to your surgery. Let's pause for a moment there and we'll talk to Mark about his particular problem in a moment.

Part Two

I   So, are you ready to see the osteopath? Is your courage up?

M   My courage is up. My, actually, it's appropriate we've come today because I'm in quite a bit of pain with my back. So, yes I'm ready, you know I'm willing and able!

I   Right, well let's eavesdrop a little on the kind of consultation that there might be between practitioner, in this case Martin, and patient Mark, and find out a little bit more about how treatment in osteopathy might work. Martin – over to you.

MM   Well, first of all I can assure you you don't have a disc problem, but we'll come to that later on. What I'd like to do is just ask you a few questions about your current health and a few questions abou the history of the problem you've had. Now, first of all, I'd like you to tell me when the first back pains started to occur.

M   You want me to go back as far as I can remember?

M   Yes please.

M   I would think in my early teens, at school.

MM   As a result of anything?

M   Well, as I was saying to Jane, I used to be in the rugby scrum and the cricket and in all the sporting events going, so, you know all these years on it's difficult to remember but one would think that that's probably where the original problem was related to.

MM   And is the pain you have in your back now similar to the pain you had then?

M   No. The pain I had then would have been sort of, it might've hurt for a while but it would've gone away again. The pain I have now is a fairly constant nagging ache, if you like. And at times if I stand for any period of time, for any length of time, then I do find I need support – it becomes extremely painful with shooting pains or whatever down my leg.

MM   I'd like to establish what treatment have you had, or did you have in your early teens for this problem, or did you just let it ride?

M   When I was younger I just let it ride. I might've rubbed in one of the, you know, the creams that you can put on a back but that would've been about it when I was younger.

MM   Now, I'd like to, I'd like to ask: When is the problem at its worst?

M   Normally towards the end of a day, after I've been on my back, or I've been walking, using my back if you like, for the day. Sometimes first thing in the morning, just literally getting out of bed can be very painful. And certainly if I sit in a slightly hunched position, which I tend to do at work, leaning forward, or at a meal table, then it's very difficult to actually stand up straight for a while afterwards.

MM   Now can you tell precisely where the pain is in your back?

M   Yes I can. This isn't going to be very good to the listeners, but it's in the lower right hand side. That's where the acute pain is, but it aches across.

MM   And are you getting any pains anywhere else that you may or may not think are related to this problem?

M   In the last couple of weeks or so I've been waking up with a stiff neck sometimes in the morning. I don't know whether that's related or whether I've got the wrong pillows, or what. But yes, sometimes I have a bit of a stiff neck. I sound a terrible crock, don't I?

MM   Now, having established that there doesn't appear to be anything wrong with you, what I'd like to do is have a closer inspection of your back, including taking your blood pressure and listening to your heart and lungs. So I'd like you to go behind the screen and slip your things off please.

I   And whilst Mark is doing that, we'll take a break.

▶ Another crime statistic (p. 206)

PC = Policeman AC = Anna Clark

Part 1

PC   Good morning. . . . Miss Clark?

AC   Yes. You're here quickly.

PC   I believe you reported a break-in.

AC   Yes. Come in. . . I got home and found the front door open. Someone's forced it. . . . look at this footprint on it. . .

PC   And is anything missing? Have you had a look to see if anything's been taken?

AC   I don't know. I don't think so. The only room they went into was my bedroom as far as I can tell. Look, sorry, come through and have a look. I'm afraid it's a bit of a mess – I left it like this, though, – it hasn't been ransacked! The only thing that's been moved, as far as I can tell, is that box over on the dressing table.

PC   Which? This Japanese-type one?

AC   Yes. It's just got a few earrings and things in it.

PC And are they all here?

AC Well, as far as I can remember, yes. It's odd – there are these two watches here, you'd think they'd have picked them up.

PC They wouldn't normally take jewellery unless it's of value. . . . Have you touched anything in here since you came in?

AC I, no. . . . Well, I picked up a few things off the floor.

PC Aha. . .

AC Wait a minute, though. I think there might a brooch missing. Let me look. . . . Yes, they must have taken it! Oh well, I suppose it was too much to hope for that I'd get away completely unscathed.

PC Was it valuable?

AC Not particulary in money terms, but it was of sentimental value.

PC Yes, I can quite understand. Well, I'll take some details about that later. Have you checked your petty cash?

AC My what?

PC You know, cash that you keep around the house?

AC Oh, there wasn't any.

PC And what about your cheque book? Where do you keep it?

AC Gosh! I hadn't thought of that. Hang on. I keep it in my desk. . . . No. It's OK. It's still here. That's a relief, I hadn't thought about that.

PC What about credit cards?

AC No that's alright. I had it with me in my purse. Look, do you think they'll come back? I can only assume that they'd just got in and come into the bedroom when they saw me drive back – that's my car in front of the window – which is why they left empty-handed.

PC Well. . . . hard to say. . . . they're usually after videos, microwaves, computers, things like that. Got anything like that?

AC What me? I have got a television but it's black and white. And an elderly stereo system.

PC I don't imagine they'd be interested in things like that. Who knows – they're in and out very quickly and they're after stuff that they know they can get rid of easily.

Part 2

PC If I could take down a few details for the record. . . .

AC Right, yes. Come through to the sitting room. Sorry about the mess, hang on, I'll move that so you can sit down. I was coming back to tidy up. I expect they took one look at the state of the place and thought it had been done over already! I'm just. . .

PC Right, if I could have a few details. First your full name?

AC Clark. C.L.A.R.K. Anna Jane.

PC Is that Miss or Mrs?

AC Ms.

PC Fine, and your date of birth? You don't have to answer that, I'll put 'declined to answer' if you'd prefer.

AC No, it's OK. 31st of the 5th, fifty four.

PC And the full address here?

AC 36 Acton Road, Redfield.

PC Right. And are you on the telephone here?

AC Yes, it's 426700.

PC Uhum. So you got home and found the front door open. What time was that?

AC Let me think. . . right. I went out at about ten. . . to the supermarket, drove back. . . so, it must have been about 11.15.

PC So the break-in must've occurred between those two times. And you parked and came in?

AC Well, I lifted the box of stuff from the boot, had a chat with my neighbour who was passing. Horrible thought! They must have been standing about two metres away watching through the window. Anyway, they didn't leave via the front, so they

must've jumped over the wall at the back of the house and gone through the trees there. You can cut through to Chester Avenue down there.

PC Is there another door to the flat?

AC No just the front door – well, I say front door, but it's actually at the side, isn't it? I have sole use of that door. The other flats upstairs all share the door at the front of the building. But, sorry. . . what did you ask me? Oh, right, no I didn't come in. When I saw the front door open and the damage to the lock, I pushed it open and shouted 'hello' in case they were still in here. I didn't want to come in until I was sure the place was empty.

PC Understandable.

AC So I went next door to ask if my neighbour had seen anything but she'd only just got in. Anyway, she kindly came back with me and stayed while I checked there was no-one in here and then I rang you.

PC We'll have a record of the time you rang. . . . what's the date today?

AC The 7th.

PC That's right. The 7th of May. Now, if I could just check that I've got the facts right. You returned at approximately 11.15 am and found that the door had been forced open and as far as you can see, the only thing which has been taken is a brooch. What would you say the value was?

AC Oh I don't know. Not much. About £50 I suppose.

PC And can you describe it?

AC Well, it was an oval shape. . . only made of glass but it was an antique – an aunt gave it to me.

PC Right, antique. I think I've got that. By the way, you'll need my name for your insurance claim. I'm PC West. . . and my number is 1690. OK?

Part 3

PC So, I think that's all I need for now, Miss Clark. I'll just take a look at the door again. . . . it looks as though they've forced a knife down the side of the lock. I'd suggest getting another lock fitted. This one's damaged and at the best of times, this type's not particularly secure, you need a mortice lock.

AC Mhm. I suppose I could get one on the insurance. A similar thing happened last year and I had to replace the whole door, and the insurance company footed the bill. . .

PC And you'll need to get the door frame fixed.

AC What? Where? Oh, I hadn't noticed that.

PC Yes, you can see it split where they kicked the door. That won't be secure now – you should get it made secure as soon as possible.

AC I'll try and get someone today. . . I don't fancy sleeping here with all and sundry able to walk in!

PC I don't think it's worth sending our Scene of the Crime people round. They're the finger print people – you'd disturbed things and I don't think they'd be able to get much.

AC Well, there's that enormous footprint on the door!

PC Yes, but that could be one of thousands. Not much use on its own.

AC I find it impossible to believe that a door can be kicked open in broad daylight without anyone seeing anything!

PC But they do it so quickly. They're purely opportunist – they see a weak lock, check there's no-one at home, and that's it. One last point before I speak to the neighbours. Have you any ideas who may have done it?

AC What? Someone I know?

PC It could be someone who bears you a grudge for some reason. Can you think of anyone like that?

AC Well not as far as I know. No, I'm sure it's no-one I know. It can't be.

PC You'd be surprised – these things do happen. I'll be off now. If you discover anything else has gone or you want to add anything to your statement, ring the police station. Whoever answers the phone will take a message and add it to the file.

AC Thanks.

PC You're welcome. Goodbye.

▶ Acquiring New Skills (p. 208)

A = Interviewer L = Lindsay

Part 1

A Right Lindsay, Sue said you're doing this course at the moment.

L Well in fact I've just finished it. It was something – it just lasted for three weeks. It was two days a week for three weeks so in fact I have just finished this thing. It was at the – what's called the Women's Workshop and it was a free course for women and I saw it advertised in the paper, I was just interested to find out what they had on offer. And so I phoned them up, and they sent me all their information. And the one I've just done was called home maintenance. . .

A Yes.

L Which. . . . taught you skills that perhaps you wouldn't learn at school being female but perhaps, I don't know the sort of things boys might be are taught at school but women aren't.

A Do these courses have specific entry requirements, at all?

L Female.

A That's the only one?

L Mhm. Yes, there seems to be no, well there's no educational requirements, there's no minimal. . .

A You don't have to have a practical bent at all?

L No. And I should imagine it's. . . a lot people who go there have never done anything practical before, which is the reason for going in. . .

A Yes.

L The first place. I don't, as far as I know there are no requirements, it just, the information I received just said, you know, there were courses for women, and they run at various times and on different days and you phone up and sign on for what you'd like to do.

Part 2

A And what sort of things, I mean, three weeks is quite a short time for that kind of course isn't it? Did it cover specific areas in detail?

L We did, now then, let me think, the first week, well the first two days rather, we were using things like power tools, electric drills, how to drill into solid walls, masonry and stone work. Or how to drill into. . . and attach things to partition walls, you know these ones with a cavity in them. . .

A Yes.

L Which then led on to putting up shelves and in fact we, they're moving into a new office so they used us to put up the new shelves for them. So that was the first couple of days. Let me think, and then the second week was glazing which was quite nerve-wracking at first; you're confronted with sheets of glass and you think you're going to cut your hands off or something. In fact, once you've got the technique it's a very simple procedure so. . .

A That's what they always say though, isn't it?

L And the same time, same week we did tiling. . . which. . . I'd always thought was an incredibly difficult thing to do but again, once you've got the basic technique and how to cut tiles and shape them and how to position things on the wall so it looks even and everything. . . What did we do? Now the last week we went on to plumbing. . .

A Aha.

L Which. . . I'd never considered doing before. And then we started off looking at the basic system of water in a house

and how it operates. And then things like how you'd mend a burst pipe.

A Yes.

L Which we did.

A Very useful.

L Yes, and that was with a blow torch which I found quite terrifying at first I thought this thing was going to, I don't know, explode in my hands or something. But in fact, again, once you'd been shown how to do it and had a go at it yourself, you found it to be a very straightforward procedure. And again something where you'd save huge amounts of money if you have a burst pipe. And in fact on the last day we installed a new telephone which, I shall be surpised if it ever works but we did it. What else did we do? Oh we did. . . fitting locks. I never knew it took so long to fit a lock. It took us hours to do it, a mortice lock.

A Yes. What about wiring? Did you do anything to do with electricity?

L Yes, we did a bit, that was on the last day, in fact. She assumed that we could all change a plug. And then we looked at things like how to put in a new lamp holder and how to change the ceiling rose or how to move a light from the centre of the room. And also we looked at switches, so that if a switch wasn't working how to take it apart and. . .

A Yes

L Check that. And obviously we had to look at a fuse box.

A Right.

L And check how to turn off the mains, so that we didn't kill ourselves doing these things. What else did we do with electricity? Mending a fuse. . . and. . .

A I suppose there's a limited amount you can do without getting too technical, isn't there?

L Yes, because then you get down to things like rewiring, which we didn't cover. Far too big a job, and I should imagine we'd need much more information to do something like that.

Part 3

A Do they do, do they run other courses?

L Yes. Yes, they do car maintenance which is eight days, which I hope to do in the future. . .

A Again, only for women?

L Only for women. Basic car maintenance and, what else do they do? There's a computer course which doesn't actually run at that centre that's, takes place somewhere else. And. . . there's woodwork and carving which they do which I may do although I'm not particularly interested in woodwork and carving. Might be useful though.

▶ Your friendly local radio station (p. 210)

Signature tune 'The best one in Bristol with all that you need to know. Good Morning'.

And a very good morning to you. It's 8.08 now on Friday morning – the weekend just around the corner. It's the 15th of January, Steve Orchard with you on the breakfast show. GWR am through till 9 o'clock and then Trevor Fry's here with the morning show. And this is Whitney Houston.

There are more breakfast shows than we used to have, on GWR, because we want to cover the area properly, we want to give each area its own identity, and in a curious way, the coming together of Radio West and Wiltshire Radio enabled there to be not less but more local radio because we were able to put more resources away from administration and more behind the microphone. So that means that we can concentrate more on local news and information and the sort of things people want to listen about their locality, and what's going on around the world as well, in the Wiltshire area and of course in the Bristol area and now a separate programme in the Bath area.

GWR Radio Bath – FM 103

7.25 Monday morning in Bath – David Preever with news and music until 9 o'clock.

GWR am with Stephen and Simon. 13 minutes to 8. Coming next 'Take Two': Swindon Town hope to roast the Canaries in the FA Cup Replay.

We've got to go to Norwich now on Wednesday night and there's no reason why we shouldn't. . . .

If anything, the Wiltshire-based breakfast programme has more speech in it than the Bristol and Bath breakfast programmes do, simply because the pace of life seems to be faster in the cities than it is in the country. And there are two people involved, of course, in the Wiltshire one and there's the interplay between the two characters which takes more time to get over than the simple exposition of one character from Steve Orchard or from David Preever.

When you wake up at breakfast time, there's a certain amount of information that you need, or you feel you need. Very basic information like the weather, traffic information, public transport information and news. So really it's, it's like a, it is a montage of moving information, getting people set up for the day, and helping them to wake up, really.

The difference, I think, between Bath and Bristol – when I first came to the area over a year ago, somebody said to me that Bath is the posh suburb of Bristol, and I think there's a danger in thinking of Bath and Bristol as both being in the West Country and I think you have to treat the two as being two very separate areas, even though they're only 8 or 9 miles apart.

The format is designed that, in such a way that we don't expect people to listen for the three hours that the breakfast show lasts. So there'll be a bit of repetition.

The idea of the pace of the programme is to fit in with the pace of people's mornings and we reckon that probably people aren't doing any one thing for more than two or three minutes in the average morning. They're sort of gulping down a bowl of cereal, getting the kids off to school, so you don't want to do anything for more than two or three minutes at a time, otherwise people will miss the end of what you're doing.

People always ask how on earth do you manage to be so bright at that time in the morning and it's simply getting a head start on everybody else. We just happen to have got up earlier than everybody else and so therefore we're into our stride earlier than everybody else.

When we're on air I haven't got much to say to people, who work with us and who help produce the programme. I haven't got much sort of cheeriness in me, apart from when the microphone opens. It's like you have three hours in the morning to use all your cheerfulness in the day up, because that's your job really, and after that you haven't got much left really.

The trouble with doing an early show, I think you find is that you have to have a huge ego because getting out of bed at four-thirty in the morning, which is a very unnatural time – I read somewhere once that you're at your lowest ebb at about half four – five in the morning – so to get out of bed at that time and then talk to yourself in a room for three hours with nobody

laughing at what you say except yourself, the only way to survive is to be a total egotist.

Music.

▶Something to complain about (p. 211)

L = Lindsay J = Jenny

L   Yes, I mean, this whole business of complaining. You're made to feel, you know, that you're being such a nuisance, how dare you. . .
J   I know.
L   Go back? And there you are, you're parted with your money to buy something and you go back when there's a fault and they're just not interested. I had. . . .
J   I know, it's amazing.
L   The, I bought one of those. . jug kettles. . . .
J   Mhm.
L   You know, the sort of plastic, new style things. And. . I noticed that there was sometimes a bit of water by it on the worktop where I keep it in the kitchen and initially I just thought, 'Oh it's a bit of condensation when I take the lid off.'
J   Yeah.
L   So I didn't really take much notice. And then, after a week or so, there was slightly more water. I thought: 'This is very odd.' And then finally, (I'm very slow) anyway, I finally realised that, in fact water was emptying from the bottom of the kettle. I thought, this is interesting and it was, there's a sort of gauge at the side at the bottom, there's a little 'L' shaped plastic piece and obviously it was slightly loose so there was a bit of water coming out of that.
J   Yeah.
L   And so it was very slow initially, just a few drops, but it started to increase the quantity of water. Anyway. So I found the receipt, didn't I, traipsed off back to the place I'd bought it from. And. . . went in and said: 'My kettle leaks from the bottom.' And. . it was something like a month out of the guarantee, it was a one year guarantee.
J   Oh.
L   And so they didn't want anything to do with it at all and I said. . .
J   I suppose, legally, they don't have to, do they?
L   Well I don't know, I argued, my argument was loud and clear, my argument was that there was some sort of design fault with this. . .
J   Yes.
L   And that the leak was a result of the way it was manufactured not the way I used it. . . .
J   Yes.
L   And given that I live alone it's not used heavily. And so. . . I felt they should show slightly more interest in this rather than just saying it's nothing to do with us.
J   Mhm.
L   And. . . the manager eventually. . . yes, the first assistant I spoke to did this total blank, she said: 'It's nothing do with us now, it's out of guarantee.'
J   Mhm.
L   So I stood there and said: 'Well look, it's absolutely no use to me as it is, it leaks from the bottom, you know, it cannot be used, it empties. . .' – I exaggerated rather – said it, you know, 'emptied as quickly as you filled it'.
J   All over the kitchen floor.
L   Yes. Anyway she finally got the manager who. . . to get rid of me said that he would contact their head office which he said he would. . .
J   They're very good at saying these things.
L   Yes oh yes.

J To get rid of you, aren't they?

L And so. . .

J Anything to get you out of the shop.

L Anyway, he got me out of the shop and then he contacted me or I contacted him the following week. And his head office had said that it was nothing to do with them because it leaked from the bottom and it was out of guarantee so nothing, not their problem.

J Mhm.

L So by this time I'd got my teeth into this, I refused to give up. All I wanted, I think if somebody had said: 'Oh it must be a nuisance having a kettle that leaks from the bottom, we do sympathise.'

J Yes.

L I would have given up and just bought another one but because nobody was in the least bit bothered or interested or kind about it I thought: 'Right; I'm going,' you know, 'I'm going to get something out of this.' So they said, write to the manufacturer's. So I wrote to the manufacturer's explaining that it was, you know, what had happened, that I'd been to the people I'd bought it from and they told me to refer it to them. They sent me back. . . this really tatty photocopy which was nothing to do with my letter.

J Oh.

L It was something about 'Thank you' – it was one of these, you know, form letters. . . .

J Yeah.

L Terribly blurred, obviously been photocopied about ten thousand times; 'Thank you for your enquiry regarding spare parts, we refer you to the local'. . . . whatsit. . . .

J That's helpful.

L Agents, I suppose they'd be, the local agents. So I was furious about this

J Mhm.

L I had troubled to write this letter which for some reason they returned to me.

J What, your letter?

L Yes, so I got back this envelope with a totally irrelevant response with my letter.

J With your letter.

L So I thought, 'Right. This is it!' So I then phoned the manufacturer's in Birmingham or somewhere like that. Vast expense, you know, telephoning during office hours. . . .

J Mhm.

L And got through to customer services department. In fact, initially I'd trouble even doing that because the letter they'd sent me was so out of date it had the wrong telephone number on, this photocopied thing. So I got through, eventually to this woman who, in fact, was terribly pleasant which amazed me, and I said, 'I'm now complaining not only about the kettle but also about the way your complaints department have handled my complaint.' So she said would I return to her my original letter, their response and a covering note. . . .

J Yes.

L To remind her what the situation was. . . .

J Mhm.

L Which I did. And then I got back from them, this is wonderful, I got this. . . letter saying: 'Because we have handled this so badly, you can have a complimentary repair done at the local agent's.' So I rushed down there with my leaking kettle and it was repaired in two days.

J Oh, that's good. It shows it is worth complaining, doesn't it? You know sometimes you just think it's not worth the bother I. . . .

L Yes.

J I'm fighting these huge forces. . .

L Yes.

J Of corporations. . .

L Who aren't interested.

J Who aren't interested.

L Yes.

J Yeah, and it's just not worth the bother but I think it is as long as you are adamant enough, and as long as you make enough of a nuisance of yourself.

▶ Acknowledgements

I would like to express my special thanks to Robert O'Neill for his encouragement at the inception of this project, to Alan Duff for his invaluable advice on the teacher's notes, and to Louise Aylward and Matthew Hancock, my superb editors, for their professionalism, insight and inexhaustible patience.

Collins ELT
8 Grafton Street
London W1X 3LA

© Sue O'Connell 1984, 1989

10 9 8 7 6 5 4 3 2 1

First published 1984
This revised and enlarged edition
First published 1989

Printed in Great Britain by Scotprint Ltd, Edinburgh

ISBN 0 00 370269 3